# MY LIFE

# MARC CHAGALL
# MY LIFE

**PETER OWEN**
London and Chester Springs

PETER OWEN PUBLISHERS
73 Kenway Road, London SW5 0RE

Peter Owen books are distributed in the USA by
Dufour Editions Inc., Chester Springs, PA 19425–0007

First published in Great Britain 1965
© Estate of Marc Chagall 1957, 1965, 1995, 2003
This paperback edition published 2003

ISBN 0 7206 1186 5

A catalogue record for this book is available from
the British Library

Printed and bound in Great Britain by
Bookmarque Ltd, Croydon, Surrey

*to my parents*
*to my wife*
*to my native town*

# Illustrations
*(on separate pages)*

# I

The first thing that caught my eye was a trough. Simple, square, half hollow, half oval. A market trough. Once inside, I filled it completely.

I do not remember now – perhaps it was my mother who told me – but just at the moment of my birth a great fire broke out in a little house near the road behind the prison on the outskirts of Witebsk.

The town was ablaze, the quarter where the poor Jews lived.

They carried the bed and mattress, the mother and the baby at her feet, to a safe place at the other end of the town.

But, most important of all, I was still-born.

I did not want to live. Imagine a white bubble that does not want to live. As if it were stuffed with pictures by Chagall.

They prick it with pins, they plunge it into a bucket of water. At length it gives a feeble whimper.

Indeed, I was still-born.

I should not like psychologists to draw the wrong conclusion from that. Heaven forbid!

However, the little house near the Peskowatik Road still stands intact. I saw it, not long ago.

My father sold it as soon as he was a little better off. It reminds me of the lump on the head of the rabbi in green whom I painted, or a potato thrown into a barrel of herrings and soaked in the brine. Looking down on this little house from my new-found "stature", I winced and asked myself, "How could I possibly have been born in there? How can one breathe in such a hole?"

But when my grandfather with the long black beard died an honourable death, my father bought another place for a few roubles.

No lunatic asylum in the neighbourhood now, as in Peskowatik. Churches, fences, shops, synagogues stand on every side, simple and eternal as the buildings in Giotto's frescoes.

Around me, all kinds of Jews, old ones, young ones, Javitches, Bejlines, come and go, turn and turn again, or simply trot along. A beggar runs toward his house, a rich man goes home. The "Cheder" boy runs home. Papa goes home.

In those days there was still no cinema.

People went home or to the shop. That's what I remember besides the trough.

I say nothing of the sky and stars of my childhood.

They are my stars, my sweet stars; they accompany me to school and wait for me in the street till I return. Poor things, forgive me. I have left you alone up there at such a dizzy height!

My sad, my joyful town!

As a boy, I would watch you from our doorstep, childlike. To a child's eyes you were so clear. When the fence blocked my view, I would climb on to a little wooden post. If I still could not see you, I would climb up on to the roof. Why not? Grandfather used to climb up there too.

And I would gaze at you as long as I liked.

There in Pokrovakaja Street, I was born for the second time.


Have you ever seen one of those men in Florentine paintings with an untrimmed beard, eyes that are both brown and ash-grey, and a complexion of burnt-ochre furrowed with lines and wrinkles?

That is my father.

Or perhaps you have seen one of those figures from the Haggadah, with their silly expressions. (Forgive me, little father!)

You remember I made a study of you. Your portrait should have given the impression of a candle flaring up and burning out at the same moment. Its aroma, the aroma of sleep.

A fly is buzzing – curse it! Because of it, I fall asleep.

Must I speak of my father?

What is a man's worth if he is worth nothing? If he is priceless? That is why it is difficult for me to find the right words to describe him.

My grandfather, a teacher of religion, could think of nothing better than to place my father – his eldest son, still a child – as a clerk with a firm of herring wholesalers, and his youngest son with a barber.

No, my father was not a clerk, but, for thirty-two years, a plain workman.

He lifted heavy barrels, and my heart used to twist like a Turkish pretzel as I watched him carrying those loads and stirring the little herrings with his frozen hands. His fat employer stood by like a stuffed animal.

Sometimes my father's clothes would glisten with herring brine. The light played above him, beside him. But his face, now yellow, now clear, would sometimes break into a wan smile.

What a smile! Where did it come from?

It blew in from the street where shadowy passers-by roamed, reflecting the moonlight. Suddenly, I saw the glint of his teeth. They reminded me of a cat's teeth, a cow's teeth, any teeth.

Everything about my father seemed sad and full of enigma. An inaccessible image.

Always tired, always worried, the only glimmer lay in his blue-grey eyes.

In his greasy, work-soiled clothes, with a dull-red handkerchief hanging out of one of his great pockets, he would come home, tall and lean. The evening came in with him.

He would pull little cakes and frozen pears out of his pockets and share them out among us children with his wrinkled brown hand. Popped into our mouths, they were more delicious, more savoury and ethereal than if they had come from the dish on the table.

And an evening without cakes and pears from Papa's pockets was a sad evening for us. I was the only one who really knew him – that simple heart, poetical and blunted with silence.

To the very last "expensive" years of his life he only made a few roubles or so. Small tips from buyers added little to his budget. And yet my father had not been a poor young man.

The photograph of him as a young man and my own observation of our wardrobe convinced me that when he married my mother he had certain physical and financial resources, since he offered his fiancée – a slip of a girl who went on growing after her marriage – a magnificent shawl.

When he married he stopped handing his wages over to his father, and ran his own home.

But first I would like to complete the figure of my bearded grandfather. I do not know whether he went on teaching for long. They say he was a highly respected man.

On visiting his grave in the cemetery ten years ago with my grandmother and seeing his monument, I was convinced that he was an honourable man. A man beyond price, a saint.

He lies quite close to the river by the black fence where the troubled waters flow. Below the hill, beside other "saints" long dead.

Though well-worn, his gravestone still stands, engraved with the Hebrew words: "Here lies . . ."

My grandmother pointed it out to me. "Here is the grave of your grandfather, your father's father, and my first husband."

She mumbled the words through her lips, unable to weep. Whispered words for herself, or prayers. I listened to her lamenting as she bent over the gravestone, as though that stone and the little mound of earth were my grandfather himself, as though grandmother were appealing to the very bowels of the earth, or the grave were a cupboard where an object lay sealed up for ever.

"I implore you, David, pray for us. This your Bathsheba. Pray for your sick son Shati, for your weak Zussy, for their children. Pray that they may be upright before God and men."

On the other hand, I was closer to my grandmother. The good woman was nothing more than a head-shawl, a little skirt, and a wrinkled face.

She was hardly four feet tall.

The love in her heart was dedicated to her few favourite children and her prayer-book.

Once a widow, she re-married, with the rabbi's blessing, my other grandfather, my mother's father, himself a widower. The former couple had died in the year of my parents' marriage. My mother ascended the throne.

## 2

My heart will always ache – is it weariness or a sudden
memory? – on the anniversary of her death, when I visit
her grave, my mother's grave.

I seem to see you, Mamma.

You come softly towards me. So slowly that I want to
help you. You smile my smile. Ah! that smile, my own.

My mother was born at Lyozno where I painted the
priest's house, the fence in front of the house, and the pigs
in front of the fence.

Pope or no pope, he smiles as he passes by, his cross
gleaming, ready to make the sign over me. He rubs his
hand on his hip. The pigs scamper out like puppies to
meet him.

My mother was the eldest daughter of the grandfather who spent half his life lying on the stove, a quarter in the synagogue, and the rest in the butcher's shop. He spent so much time resting that my grandmother succumbed and died in the prime of her life.

It was then that grandfather started to stir. So the cows and the calves stirred too.

Was my mother really so short?

Father married her without looking at her first.

But that is a mistake.

In our eyes, mother had a style that was rare, as far as was possible in such a commonplace environment.

But I do not wish to praise or overpraise my mother who is no more. Can I speak of her at all?

At times, I would rather not speak, but sob.

I rush through the cemetery gate. Lighter than a flame, an aerial shadow, I hasten to shed my tears.

I see the river flowing away into the distance, the bridge beyond, and close at hand, the eternal barrier, the earth, the grave.

Here is my soul. Look for me here; here I am, here are my pictures, my roots. Sadness, sadness!

That is her portrait.

What does it matter? Is it not my own also? Who am I?

You will smile, passing stranger, you will be amazed, you will laugh.

A lake of suffering, hair prematurely grey, eyes—a world of tears, a soul that hardly exists, a brain that is no more.

What is there, then?

I can see her ruling the whole house, directing my father, endlessly building little houses, starting a grocer's shop, bringing in a cartload of goods bought on credit. What words, what means can I use to portray her smiling at the doorway, or seated for hours at the table, ever waiting for some neighbour to whom she might unburden her soul?

In the evening when the shop was shut, and all the

children were home, Papa dozed over the table, the lamp rested and the chairs grew bored; outside, you could hardly tell where the sky was or where nature had vanished. Not that we were silent, but everything was quiescent. Mamma would sit in front of the tall stove, one hand on the table, the other on her stomach.

Her head rose to a point at the top where her hair was fastened with a pin. She would tap her finger several times on the table covered with an oilcloth, which meant, "Everybody's asleep. What children! I've no-one to talk to!"

She loved talking. She fashioned her words so well that the listener became embarassed and smiled.

Queen-like, erect, and motionless, her pointed coiffure immaculate, she would put questions, fall silent, or speak, her lips scarcely moving. But there was no-one there. Only myself, following her from a distance.

She would ask: "Talk to me, my son."

I am a little boy, and Mamma is a queen. What can I say?

She is cross, and drums her fingers on the table.

And the house is wrapped in a veil of sadness.

On Fridays, after the Sabbath dinner when my father invariably fell asleep, always at the same moment, the prayer unfinished, (on my knees before you, Papa!), her eyes would grow sad, and she would say to her eight children: "Children, let us sing the rabbi's song, help me!"

The children would sing and fall asleep. She would then begin to cry and I would say: "There you go again, I won't sing any more."


What I meant was that my talent was hidden somewhere in her, that everything came to me through her, except her spirit.

There she is at my door (at Javitch's, in the courtyard). She knocks and asks:

"Are you there, my son? What are you doing? Has Bella been to see you? Do you want something to eat?"

"Look, Mamma, how do you like that?"

She looks at my painting, with God only knows what eyes!

I await the verdict. At last she says slowly:

"Yes, my boy, I see; you have talent. But listen to me, child. Perhaps you ought to be a clerk. I feel sorry for you. With your shoulders. Where do you get that talent?"

She was not only our mother but also mother to her own sisters. When one of them got engaged, it was my mother who decided whether or not the young man was suitable. She it was who judged, investigated, enquired. If the young man lived in another town, she would go there, and as soon as she had his address, she would make for the shops opposite, buy something, and enter into conversation. And when night fell, she would even try to peep through the window into the young man's house.


So many years have slipped by, since she died!

Where are you now, little mother? In heaven, on earth? I am here, far from you. I would be happier if I had been closer to you; at least I would have seen your monument, touched your gravestone.

Ah! Mamma. I can no longer pray, and I weep less and less. But my soul thinks of you, of myself, and my thoughts are consumed in grief.

I do not ask you to pray for me. You know yourself what my sorrows may be. Tell me, little mother: from the other world, from Paradise, from the clouds, from where you are, does my love comfort you?

Can I spin any sweet, tender comfort for you with my words?

## 3

In the graveyard at her side lie other women from Mohileff
or Lyozno. Hearts at rest. Broken hearts, colds of one kind
or another. I know them. It is always the same courage,
the courage that killed my rosy young grandmother, who
worked herself to death while grandfather spent his days
in the synagogue or on the stove. The same miraculous
courage shown after the fast on the Day of Atonement, on
a moonlit evening, towards the New Year.

Dear old man – so young!

How I loved you when I was at Lyozno in your rooms,
which smelt of tanned cowhide! I loved your sheepskins.
Your entire wardrobe always hung in the entry, on the
door, and the coatstand with the coats, the hats, the whip

and the rest, made a distinct silhouette, which I have never studied properly, against the grey background of the wall. All that was my grandfather.

In his stable there is a big-bellied cow; she stands and stares stubbornly.

Grandfather goes up and talks to her like this:

"Hey, listen, give us your legs. You must be tied up. We need something to sell, meat, do you hear?"

She falls with a sigh.

I reach out to put my arms round her muzzle, to whisper a few words to her -- that she shouldn't worry, I won't eat the meat; what more could I do?

She hears the rye rippling, and she sees the blue sky behind the hedge.

But the butcher, in black and white, knife in hand, is rolling up his sleeves. The prayer is hardly over before he holds her neck back and runs the steel into her throat.

Torrents of blood.

Impassively, the dogs and hens wait around for a drop of blood, a morsel that might accidentally fall to the ground.

Nothing can be heard but their clucking, their rustling, and grandfather's sighs amid the torrents of fat and blood.

And you, little cow, naked and crucified, you are dreaming in heaven. The glittering knife has raised you to the skies.

Silence.

The intestines uncoil and the pieces fall apart. The skin drops off.

Pink, blood-red pieces pour out. Steam rises.

What a job to have on one's hands!

I feel like eating meat.

Every day two or three cows were killed like this, and the fresh meat was offered to the owner of the estate and to the other tenants.

For me, my grandfather's house was full of the sounds and smells of art.

It was only from the hides, hung up to dry like linen.

In the dark of the night, it seemed to me that there were not only smells, but a whole flock of blessings, breaking through the boards, flying into space.

The cows were slaughtered cruelly. I excused it all. The skins dried piously, offering tender prayers, praying the heavenly ceiling to forgive the sins of their slaughterers.

My grandmother always fed me with meat that was specially roasted, grilled, or baked. What was it? I didn't know exactly. Maybe the stomach, neck, ribs, liver, or lungs. I didn't know.

For in those days I was particularly stupid and, it seems to me, happy.

Grandfather, I still remember you.

One day, coming across a sketch of a nude woman, he turned away from it, as if it was no concern of his, or as if it were a strange star in the market place that had nothing to do with the inhabitants. And then I understood that my grandfather, as well as my wrinkled little grandmother, thought nothing of my art (what an art, that does not even convey a likeness) and set a very high value on meat.

This is what my mother told me about her father, my grandfather from Lyozno. Or perhaps I dreamt it.

The feast of Sukkot or Simchat Torah.

They look for him everywhere.

Where is he, where is he?

It turned out that because of the fine weather we were having, grandfather had climbed on to the roof, sat down on the chimney-pots, and was regaling himself on carrots. Not a bad picture.

I do not mind if people, with joy and relief, discover the enigma of my pictures in these innocent adventures of my relatives.

How little that matters to me! My dear fellow-citizens, you are welcome!

If for posterity you need proof of your good judgment and my lack of common sense, I shall even tell you what my mother told me about my fine relatives from Lyozno.

One of them could find nothing better to do than to parade along the street of the quarter, wearing nothing but a shirt.

Well? Is that shocking?

The memory of that *sans-culotte* will always fill my heart with radiant joy. As if a painting by Masaccio or Piero della Francesca had come to life on the streets of Lyozno in broad daylight. I felt close to him.

I am not joking though. If my art had no place in my family's life, their lives and their achievements greatly influenced my art.

You know, I felt elated when I stood by my grandfather's place in the synagogue.

Poor unhappy child, how I twisted and turned before I arrived! Facing the window, prayer-book in hand, I surveyed the scene of the quarter as long as I liked, on the Sabbath.

Beneath the drone of prayers, the sky seemed bluer to me. The houses float in space. And every passer-by could be seen clearly.

Behind me, they are beginning the prayer, and my grandfather is asked to say it in front of the altar. He prays, he sings, he repeats it melodiously, and begins it all over again. As though an oil mill were turning in my heart. Or as though new honey, freshly gathered, were trickling down inside me.

And should he weep, I remember my unsuccessful drawing and think: Will I be a great artist?


I forgot to remember you, little uncle Neuch. With you, we used to go out into the country to fetch cattle. How happy I was when you agreed to take me with you in your jolting cart!

Somehow or other, it took us along. On the other hand, there was something to look at on every side.

Road, road, fine sandstone, and my Uncle Neuch sniffs and urges his horse on: "Hey, hey."

On the way back, I thought I ought to show more ingenuity and skill, and I pulled the cow along by the tail, begging her not to lag behind. As we crossed the plank bridge, I felt as if several wooden cutlets were rolling about in my stomach. The sound of the wheels was different.

Uncle never looked at the little river, the reeds, the fence along the bank, the mill or, farther on, the solitary little church, the small houses in the market place, which was growing dark by the time we crossed it, exhausted and I with God or I know not what in my heart.

Everyone is bargaining, and behind the counter sit young girls.

I don't understand a thing.

I have only just arrived, and they are calling out to me from their shops and smiling at me. I have curly hair. They offer me buns, sweets. Youth ripens in vain. Is that my fault? Can I tear myself apart then?


It would be more interesting to paint my sisters and my brother.

How I would be captivated by the harmony of their hair, their skin, how eagerly I would tackle them, intoxicating the canvases and you with the vapour of my thousand-year-old colours!

But to describe them! I can't promise to say more than a word about my aunts, one of whom had a long nose, a good heart, and ten children; the other, a shorter nose and half a dozen children, but she was fonder of herself – why not? The third, with a nose like a Morales painting, had three children, of whom one stuttered, one was deaf, and the third still in the process of formation.

Aunt Mariassja is the palest.

Why, being so sickly, does she live in this neighbourhood?

The moujiks tramp around in front of her house and the shop.

Herrings in barrels, oats, sugar shaped like pointed heads, flour, candles in blue wrapping – all are on sale.

The money clinks.

Moujiks, tradesmen and men of God whisper, stink.

Aunt is lying on the sofa. Her yellow hands are folded, crossed. Nails black and white. Eyes white and yellow. Her teeth gleam dimly.

Black dress that reveals her worn, outstretched body.

Her chest sags and her stomach too.

Holy sounds ring out beneath her feet.

Perhaps she will die soon, and her body will stiffen in gentle ecstasy in the suburban soil.

More than once I have dreamt that a piece of buttered bun fell out of her hands into my mouth.

I stood at the door in front of her and stared at the creases in that bun like a beggar.

Aunt Relly is not like that.

Her little nose is like a gherkin. Her little hands and breasts are tightly squeezed by her dark brown bodice.

She cackles, laughs, fiddles and fidgets.

One skirt on top of another, scarves above and below, and her teeth fly up towards hair that is a tangle of combs and pins.

She pours out the fresh cream, inviting me to taste the cheese.

Her husband is dead. Their tannery closed down. In our part of town, the goats began to cry.

And Aunts Moussia, Gouttja, Chaja!

If they had angels' wings, they would fly across the market, above the baskets of berries, pears and currants.

People look at them and ask:

"Who is it flying like that?"

I have also had half-a-dozen uncles, or more.

They were all good Jews. Some had bigger stomachs and emptier heads, some black beards, others brown.

In a nutshell, that's painting.

Every Saturday Uncle Neuch would put on a tallit, any tallit, and read the Bible aloud.

He played the violin, like a cobbler.

Grandfather listened and dreamed.

Only Rembrandt could have known what the old grandfather, butcher, tradesman and cantor thought while his son played the violin beside the window, beside the dirty window panes covered with raindrops and finger marks.

Behind the window, the night.

Only the priest is asleep and behind him, behind his house, a waste peopled with ghosts.

But uncle is playing the violin.

The man who spent the whole day leading the cows into the sheds, tying their legs, and dragging them around, is playing now, playing the rabbi's song.

What does it matter how he plays? I smile, trying my hand at his violin, pouncing at his pockets, his nose.

He buzzes, like a fly.

My head floats gently about the room on its own.

Transparent ceiling. Clouds and blue stars steal in along with the smell of the fields, the stable, and the roads.

I am sleepy.

I am content to snatch the crusts of bread and the spoon and eat my supper, shivering.


Uncle Leiba is sitting on a bench beside his country house. His daughters browse like red cows.

Uncle Juda is still on the stove.

He seldom goes out, even to the synagogue.

He prays at home, beside the window.

He mutters silently, and his sallow complexion slips to the casement window, goes down the street, and settles on the cupola of the church. He looks like a wooden house with a transparent roof.

I could have sketched him in a moment.

Uncle Israel is still sitting in the same place in the synagogue, with his arms behind his back.

He is warming himself, eyes closed, in front of the stove.

The lamp is burning on the table. A thick black shadow lies on the floor, on the altar.

He reads and rocks, rocks and sings, mutters and sighs.

Suddenly, he stands up.

"It is time for the evening prayer."

Night already! Blue stars. Violet earth.

The shops are closing.

Soon supper will be served – cheese, plates.

Why didn't I die in your house, under the table?

My uncle is afraid to offer me his hand. They say I am a painter.

Suppose I were to sketch him?

God forbids it. A sin.

I have one other uncle, Zussy; he is a hairdresser, the only one in Lyozno. He could even be a hairdresser in Paris. His manners, his moustache, his smile, his expression . . . He stayed in Lyozno. There, he was a star. There were stars on his window and on the door of his shop too. Above it, a blue sign depicting a man covered with a white cloth, with soapy cheeks, and another man busy shaving him – murdering him.

Uncle cut my hair and shaved me with pitiless affection, and boasted about me (he was the only one) throughout the entire neighbourhood, even in front of the local Squire.

When I painted his portrait and offered it to him, he glanced at the canvas then, looking at himself in the glass, reflected a little, and said,

"Well, no – keep it!"

God forgive me if I have left out of my description all that clamorous love that I have, in general, for mankind.

And my parents are the most saintly of all.
I want it that way.


The rustle of leaves. Your stones. Your graves. Hedges, troubled river, finished prayers; all that is before me.

No words. It all hides within me, writhing and soaring like your memory.

Your pallor, the thinness of your hands, your dried-up skeletons wring my heart. To whom can I pray?

How I can I beg you, beg God through you, for a shred of happiness, of joy?

I often stare into the empty blue sky, not with tears, but with pity and sadness.

You know, my parents, I am a different person already – sad, disillusioned in many things!

But enough! *Au revoir!*

# 4

Day after day, winter and summer, my father rose at six
o'clock in the morning and went off to the synagogue.

There he said his usual prayer for one dead soul or
another.

On his return, he prepared the samovar, had a drink of
tea, and left for work.

Hellish work, the work of a galley-slave.

What's the good of hiding it? How can I tell it?

No word can ease my father's lot (no sympathy, I beg
you, and above all, no pity!).

There was always plenty of butter and cheese on the
table.

Bread and butter, like an eternal symbol, was never out
of my hands when I was a child.

Wherever I went – into the courtyard, down the street,
even to the lavatory – I took a piece of bread and butter
with me, like all the others.

Were we hungry? Not at all.

It was a sort of craving. A perpetual urge to eat, dream, yawn, chew.

We particularly liked to . . . inside the fence at night.

Excuse my vulgarity! Am I vulgar?

Naturally we children were afraid of going too far away in the moonlight – we couldn't even move, our legs would not move.

Next morning, father would scold the children for their disgraceful behaviour.

I liked to sleep. Not at night, I liked to sleep in the morning, when a ray of sunlight peered in at me through the window, from below the roof.

The flies are buzzing already, and darting down on to my nose.

Oh! How much longer?

Father comes in with a strap in his hand and speaks to me:

"You do have to go to school, I suppose?"

I study the blue curtains, the cobwebby ceiling, the window and the houses, and I think:

"True, everyone does seem to be up already. You can stop scratching yourself."

I hear the dining room door open. A woman enters.

"Give me three pennyworth of good herring, please. You should have some good herring."

I wake up. I don't know what time it is. It's morning.
The tea is on the table. I am incapable of conveying its colour, its smell. The sugary liquid, followed by a roll, flows into me.


On Fridays, my father had a general wash. Mother religiously brought the pitcher of hot water from the stove and father washed himself here, there and everywhere – his head, chest, and his black hands – moaning that everything was disorganized, there was no soda left.

"A whole family of eight children – on my hands! Not a bit of help."

I choked back my tears and thought of my poor art, of my future. The steam from the hot water, combined with the smell of soap and soda, overwhelmed me.

The candles, lit in honour of the Sabbath, were cutting my throat like that cow's in my grandfather's stable.

Sanctity of the blood. It was hot and offensive.

The Sabbath dinner – my father's clean hands, his face and his white shirt – calmed me. All was well.

The meal was served. Oh! my appetite!

Stuffed fish, meat with carrots, noodles, calves-foot jelly, soup, stewed fruit, white bread. The temperature was rising.

Father fell asleep.

I always looked at him with jealousy when he was served dishes of meat and gravy, particularly roasts.

Avidly my eyes followed the stewpot, from the place it came from to the place where it stood while mother arranged the plate.

Isn't there a scrap left, even a knucklebone, that I could enjoy too?

Papa, tired and sad, seemed to have difficulty in eating. His moustache moved up and down mournfully.

I watched beside him, like a dog. I was not the only one watching.

Behind me and beside me, sitting or standing, were my younger sisters; a little farther away, my brother. All of us longed to eat roast meat out of a pot like that. Delicious!

I was thinking: Perhaps a time will come when I am a father myself, master of the house, and can eat such roast meat whenever I like.

All those Sabbath dishes carried me far, far away, bringing a certain meaning back into my life.

The last piece of meat flies from father's plate to mother's and back.

"Eat it yourself."

"You eat it!"

Father was already snoring, before he had time to say his prayer (what could one do?), and mother, in front of the stove, was singing the rabbi's song, followed by us all.

I remembered my grandfather, the cantor.

I remembered my oil mill, and I sobbed to myself, farther away from the stove, behind the curtain, at the hem of my mother's dress.

She ended the song in tears, sobbing aloud, lingering over the words.

What heart (not mine) would not have unburdened itself that night, at the thought that there was no-one on the street, only the lanterns squinting and guttersnipes p . . .

The candles burn out in the room, fade away in the sky.

They smell strong. I have a headache.

I am afraid to go out into the yard.

One day, late in the evening, I caught a thief there. She asked: "Where can I find an inn round here? I've come from the cemetery."

Everyone is going to bed. But from the direction of the market place comes the distant sound of music in the park. People are out walking there.

There, the trees caress one another, bending over in the darkness, the leaves whisper.


The night before the Sabbath, all the children gathered round the table. But during the week, Papa sat there alone drinking his tea until ten o'clock at night.

When my eldest sister, Aniouta, came back from a walk, she would go into our shop, which was on the way in, to fetch a herring, and carry it in by the tail. The younger girls, arriving later, each brought another herring in, in turn.

Herrings, gherkins, cheese, butter and a big round loaf of black bread are on the table. In the lamplight, they can hardly be seen. That is our dinner.

Magic!

On weekdays, I lived on black kasha, among other things. It was the vilest food in the world, to me.

The thought that there were grains in my mouth drove me wild, as though my mouth had been full of pistons.

It was in the days of the Soviets that I came to know and even to love millet and barley meal – particularly when a heavy bag of the stuff hung on my back.

Towards dinner time I usually fell asleep with all my clothes on, and then mother would come to wake her eldest son.

"I don't know what's the matter with him. As soon as dinner's ready, he falls asleep. Come and eat, my son!"

"What?"

"Gruel."

"Which kind?"

"Buckwheat with milk."

"I want to sleep, Mamma."

"Come and eat first."

"I don't like it."

"Come and try it first; if it chokes you, if you faint, you shan't eat any more."

I confess I sometimes fainted on purpose.

Now and then, they spared me. But that was at other times, in other places, and for other reasons.

Winter. My legs stand up, but my head is floating away. I stand in front of the black cast-iron stove and warm myself.

In front, on a chair, mother is sitting, broad and buxom, like a queen.

Papa has put the samovar on and has begun to roll cigarettes.

There's the sugar-bowl. How glad I am!

Mamma talks and talks, drums her fingers on the table, tosses back her hair.

Her tea goes cold. Papa listens, looks at his cigarette. A whole mountain of rolled cigarettes has already risen.

Night. Lying in bed, I see a silhouette on the wall – a towel, perhaps. It looks to me like a ghost, a man, an uncle wearing the tallit.

Suddenly he smiles. He turns threatening. Or else it's one of the aunts, or a goat.

I had to get up, go right to my parents' bedroom, only as far as their door, for I am afraid of going in there, especially when I see my father lying there with his beard in the air, his mouth open, snoring.

At the door I whisper:

"Mamma, I'm frightened."

A voice, dreamily:

"What do you want?"

"I'm frightened."

"Go to bed."

I calm down at once.

The little oil lamp gently takes possession of my soul and I walk slowly back to bed, where my brother David is sleeping at my feet.

Poor David! Now that he lies in the Crimea, in its earth – still so young, he who loved me so much – his name is sweeter to me than a row of horizons, and brings me the breath of my native land.

My brother. I could do nothing. Tubercular. The cypresses. Far away from us all. Decline.

But before, we used to sleep in the same bed.

At night, I seemed to see the walls closing in.

The dim lamplight cast shadows on the ceiling. I buried my face in the pillow.

Suddenly I hear a mouse behind my head. Annoyed, I catch it noisily and throw it over towards my brother's feet. He, startled in his turn, throws it back to me. In the end we both go and drown it in the chamber-pot.

The cool morning, the holy morning, is already glancing through the window panes, and we fall asleep.

When I was too frightened, my mother would call me to her.

That was the safest place.

No towel will change into a goat and an old man, and no sepulchral figure will glide across the frozen window-panes.

The drawing-room mirror, tall and dark, will frighten me no more.

Its corners and the grooves of its frame still hold the souls of my parents, now long dead, and the smiles of young girls.

Neither the hanging lamp nor the sofa will frighten me, as long as I am in Mamma's bed.

But I am afraid. She is big, with breasts as plump as pillows.

The softness of her body, from age and childbearing, the sufferings of her maternal life, the sweetness of her workaday dreams, her fat, rubbery legs — I am afraid of accidentally touching all that.

Our childhood illnesses usually began with dreams about my mother.

Night. The cold of winter. The house sleeps.

Suddenly, from the direction of the street, the silhouette of our dead grandmother Chana closes the little fanlight with a bang, saying: "Why do you leave the window open in this cold weather, my daughter?"

Or, another day, an old man all in white comes to the house, from the other world, an uncle with a long beard. Once inside, he remains standing, begs for charity. I offer him a piece of bread. Without a word, he knocks it away. The bread falls.

"Chazia," said my mother, waking up, "please go and look at the children."

That's how we used to fall ill.


Sticks and roofs, beams, fences, and everything that lay behind, delighted me.

And you can see what was there in my picture, "Above the Town". Or else, I can tell you.

A row of lavatories, little houses, windows, gateways, hens, a disused factory, a church, a little hill (an old cemetery where they bury no-one now).

I could see it in more detail from the little window of our attic, by crouching right down.

I put my head out and breathed in the cool blue air. Birds fly past me.

I hear a housewife splashing around.

I can see her stockings and her legs. She is muddying my precious pieces of broken pottery that I love so much, my stones. She is hurrying to the wedding. She has no children.

There she will weep over the fate of the bride.

I like wedding musicians, the sounds of their polkas and waltzes.

I hurry too, and I weep there beside Mamma. I like to weep a little when the badchan sings and cries in his high voice:

"Bride, bride! Think what awaits you!"

What awaits you?

At those words, my head gently detaches itself from my body and weeps somewhere near the kitchens where the fish are being prepared.

No more weeping. Enough.

Everyone blows his nose, and confetti rises in clouds, little bits of multi-coloured paper.

Congratulations! Good luck!

Grandfathers and grandmothers, young men and girls,

beggars and musicians, we all prance round, clap, and cross hands.

We kiss one another, we sing, and dance in rings.

"Congratulations!"

And whom shall I kiss?

I must find someone. After all, I can't kiss an old woman, a bearded man.

I am looking for some beauty or other.


Next to our house there were others where people scurried about.

Behind us lived a carter.

He worked at the same time as his horse. His good horse did its best to pull the loads. But it was really the carter who pulled him.

He was tall and thin, taller than his horse, longer than his cart.

When he sat there holding the reins and the whip in his hands, he looked as though he were steering a boat. But there was no wind.

Quite the opposite. It was calm, outside.

He didn't earn his living. His wife sold brandy at home (illegally), but it was that man who drank all the liquor, secretly by himself.

Then there was no more peace in our street. He couldn't sing. When he was drunk, he could only neigh in front of his horse. That horse must have laughed.

But he, forgetting his horse, would stagger along beside the cart.

Opposite us stood another house, only just in sight.

There lived Tanjka, a laundress and a thief; in the other half of the house, a chimney-sweep, with his wife and many children.

All one ever heard was their quarelling.

The voices came out of the stovepipes, near which a bucket of water was placed in case of fire.

Sometimes, after heaping insults on her husband, she would go outside for a breath of air on the bench.

When I went out at the same time, she would toss her head, which meant:

"Well, what do you think of that blighter? And he still thinks he's in the right!"

On the left, another wooden house, occupied by a man and a half.

They dealt in horses. They also stole pigeons, which they snaffled in full flight, by driving them off their roosts.

They often fought on the street.

One day, I had the impression one of them was actually trying to carry me off, although I was only a child.

Squeezed in beside the chimney-sweep were the bakers, the most distinguished family in our street.

As early as five o'clock in the morning, the lamp was burning in their window, and their stove was already warming up. It was hot in the kitchen.

Baskets were soon filled with wholesome, freshly-baked rolls. And, in the morning, I would happily run to fetch them, proudly bearing away a couple of piping hot rolls.

How terrified I was of the little girls in our neighbourhood! Childish fury reached the point when the little girl, hypnotized, followed me into the courtyard where, after tormenting each other a little, we let each other go.

I do not remember how old I was when, playing with little Olga, I refused to give her back her ball unless she showed me her leg.

"Show me your leg, up to there, and I'll give you your ball back!"

Such tricks amaze me today. And I am annoyed at their lack of success.

Yet there were days when I did not only play with sticks, dice, and feathers, nor climb around in nearby timber-

yards with my playmate, who would knock on the beams
with his . . . making me frightened.

There were days I spent entirely on the rafts.

I would bathe, get dressed, and dive in again. Only I
was rather embarrassed about getting into the water.

My schoolmate would tease me mercilessly.

"Just look what a little one he's got!"

Nothing distressed me more than that red-headed ras-
cal's jeers.

It was always the same.

Is his any better than mine if he is a great idiot, a
spoiled brat, debauched?

I am alone in the river. I bathe. I hardly disturb the water.

Around me, the peaceful town. The milky, blue-black
sky is a little bluer to the left and heavenly bliss shines
down from on high.

Suddenly, from the opposite bank, a puff of smoke shoots
out from under the synagogue roof.

As though you could hear cries from the burning scrolls
of the Torah and from the altar.

The window panes break.

Quick, out of the water!

Stark naked, I ran over the beams to get my clothes.
How I love fires!

Flames are shooting up on all sides. Half the sky is already full of smoke. It is reflected in the water.

The shops close.

Everything is on the move – people, horses, furniture.

Cries, calls, collisions.

The house where I was born becomes dearer, more
lovable to me.

I run towards it, to see it and to say goodbye.

Embers, shadows, and reflections of the fire are already
falling on the roof.

It's as though it had fainted.

My father and I, the neighbours, throw water over it,
soak it; they save it.

Towards evening, I climb on to the roof to get a better view of the burned town.

Everything is smoking, splitting apart, collapsing.

Sad and weary, I go back into the house.

# 5

In addition to my skill at playing games with sticks and feathers, bathing, and standing on roofs during fires, I had other talents.

Did you never hear my childish voice, at Witebsk?

In our courtyard there lived an old man, short and rather stout.

His long black beard, tinged with silver, was always wagging, pointing up into the air or down to the ground.

He was a teacher and a cantor.

Not particularly impressive, either as a teacher or as a cantor.

I took lessons in the rudiments and in singing from him.

Why did I sing?

Where could I have learnt that the voice is not only meant for shouting and arguing with one's sisters?

I had a voice, and I raised it as often as I liked.

In the street, all the passers-by would turn round, not

realizing that this was a song. They would say to one another:

"He must be mad, what's he got to shout about?"

I had undertaken to help the cantor and, on holy days,
the whole synagogue and I could hear the strains of my
sonorous soprano distinctly.

I saw smiles, attention, on the faces of the faithful, and
I dreamt:

"I'll be a singer, a cantor, I'll go to the Conservatory."

In our courtyard there also lived a violinist. I did not
know where he came from.

During the day, he was an ironmonger's clerk; in the
evenings, he taught the violin.

I scraped out a tune of some kind.

And no matter what or how I played, he always said,
"Admirable!", beating time with his foot.

And I thought: "I'll be a violinist, I'll go to the Conservatory."

At Lyozno, in every house, relatives, neighbours, en-
couraged me to dance with my sister. I was charming, with
my curly hair.

I thought: "I'll be a dancer, I'll go to . . ." I didn't know
where.

Night and day I wrote verses.

People spoke well of them.

I thought: "I'll be a poet, I'll go to . . ."

I no longer knew where to let myself go.

Have you seen our river, the Dvina, on autumn feast
days?

The bathing huts are dismantled. Bathing is over. It is
cold.

On the banks, the Jews are casting their sins into the
water. In the shade, a canoe is floating. You can hear the
swish of the oars.

Deep down in the water, my father's reflection is quivering, head upside down.

He also is shaking the specks of sin out of his clothes.

On those feast days, they woke me up at one or two o'clock in the morning, and I ran off to sing in the synagogue. Why does one run out like that at dead of night? I would have been far better off in bed.

In the dark, a whole crowd was hurrying towards the synagogue, staving off sleep. They will not go back to bed until they have finished the prayer.

The morning tea with cakes the colour and shape of an Oriental relic, the carefully arranged feast dishes, which had brief prayers blown over them before they could be tasted.

The dishes on the Day of Atonement, the night before.

An evening of chickens, soup.

Tall candles glow in the distance.

Soon they will be carried to the synagogue.

Those white, well-trimmed candles are already on the way, praying and pleading.

These are they that shine for the dead, for my mother, my father, my brothers, my grandfather, for all those who lie underground.

Hundreds of candles burn in the boxes of earth, like blazing hyacinths.

They flare up and blaze.

Faces, beards, white blotches, huddle together, standing, sitting, or bowed.

My father, bent and out of breath, finds the prayer-books for my mother before going to the temple and, addressing her, shows her the pages that are turned down.

"So then, from here up to there."

Sitting down at the table, he underlines the chosen pages with a pencil, with his nails.

In one corner, he writes: "Begin here."

Near one moving passage he notes: "Weep." In another place: "Listen to the cantor."

And Mamma would go to the temple assured that she would not shed tears in vain, but only in the right places.

At the worst – if she lost the thread of the prayer – she would look down from the high balcony where the women sat.

When she saw the sign "Weep" coming, she would begin to shed holy tears, like all the others. A flush came to their cheeks, and little wet diamonds trickled down drop after drop, rolling over the pages.

Papa is all in white.

Once a year, on the Day of Atonement, he looked to me like the prophet Elijah.

His face is a little yellower than usual, brick-red after the tears.

He wept unaffectedly, silently, and in the right places.

Not one extravagant gesture.

Sometimes, he would give a cry: "Ah! Ah!" turning towards his neighbours to ask them to keep silent during the prayer, or to ask them for a pinch of snuff.

As for me, I fled from the synagogue and ran towards the garden hedge. As soon as I had climbed over it, I picked a big green apple.

I took a bite of it on that fast day.

Only the blue sky saw me, sinner that I was, and my chattering teeth consumed the juice and the core of the apple.

I was not capable of keeping up the fast to the end, and that evening, in reply to Mamma's question: "Have you been fasting?" I replied, like a condemned man: "Yes."

I have no words to describe the hours of the evening prayer.

At that hour, the temple seemed to be entirely filled with saints.

Slowly, gravely, the Jews unfold their holy veils, full of tears from the whole day's prayers.

Their clothes open out like fans.

The murmur of their voices steals into the ark, whose little doors are sometimes revealed, sometimes hidden.

I am stifling. I do not move.

Endless day! Take me, make me closer to you. Speak one word, explain!

All day long I hear "Amen! Amen!" and I see them all kneeling.

"If You exist, make me blue, fiery, lunar, hide me in the altar with the Torah, do something, God, for our sake, for mine."

Our soul grows giddy, and arms are raised below the coloured windows.

The dried branches of tall poplars sway peacefully outside.

In broad daylight, little clouds turn, break, and melt away.

Soon the moon, a half-moon, will appear.

The candles have burnt right down, and the tiny lights shine today in the pure air.

Now the candle flares up to the moon, now the moon flies down to our arms.

The very road prays. The houses weep.

The sky sails past on all sides.

The stars come out and fresh air enters my open mouth.

Thus we go home.

What evening is clearer, what night more transparent than this?

Papa goes to bed tired, famished.

His sins are already forgiven, and Mamma's too.

Perhaps I am the only one who is still a bit of a sinner.

And the Passovers! Nothing—not unleavened bread, nor horse-radish—excites me so much as the Haggadah, its lines, its pictures, and the red wine in the brimming glasses. I should have liked to have drained every one of them dry.

Impossible.

Sometimes the wine in Papa's glass seemed even redder.

It reflected a deep, royal purple, the ghetto marked out for the Jewish people and the burning heat of the Arabian desert, so painfully crossed.

And the light streaming down from the hanging lamp at night, how it weighs on me!

It seemed to me I saw tents on the sands; Jews, naked in the blazing sun, argued violently about us, our existence – Moses and God.

My father, raising his glass, tells me to go and open the door.

Open the door, the outer door, so late at night, to let in the prophet Elijah?

A sheaf of white stars, silvery against the blue velvet background of the sky, enters my eyes and my heart.

But where is Elijah and his white chariot?

Is he still waiting in the courtyard, perhaps, to enter the house in the guise of a wretched old man, a hunchbacked beggar, with a pack on his back and a stick in his hand?

"Here I am. Where is my glass of wine?"


In the summer, when rich people's children go on holiday, my mother would say to me pityingly:

"Listen, son, go to Lyozno to your grandfather's for a fortnight, if you like."

A suburb, like those in the pictures.

Once again, there I am.

All the houses are there, as well as the little river, the bridge, the road.

It's all there. And the voluminous white church is there too, in the centre of the main square.

Around it, the townsfolk are selling sunflower seeds, flour, crockery.

The moujik on his cart drives casually into the town, as if he just happened to be passing through. He makes straight for one door or another.

An Oriental merchant or his ever-pregnant wife trail him, making fun of him:

"Hang you, Ivan! Don't you recognize me? Isn't there anything you need today?"

On market days, the little church was choked, crammed with people.

Moujiks on their wagons, baskets, all sorts of wares pressed in on it so closely that it seemed as though God Himself had been driven out.

All around, people were bustling, shouting, stinking. Cats were miaowing. Roosters for sale were cackling, tied up inside their baskets. Pigs were grunting. Mares were whinnying.

Brilliant colours were rioting in the sky.

But everything fell quiet towards evening.

The icons came to life, the lamps shone out again. The cows fell asleep in their sheds, snoring on the manure, and so did the hens on their rafters, blinking maliciously.

The merchants, making up their accounts, are already at the table under the lamp. Girls with round, milky breasts languish in the corners.

Try squeezing them. A white, sugary liquid will spatter your cheeks.

The clear, enchanted moon is turning behind the roofs, and I am left alone in the square, dreaming.

A transparent pig stands in front of me, its feet ecstatically buried in the earth.

I am in the street. The posts slant.

The sky is greyish-blue. The solitary trees are bowed.

How I wish I could ride a horse!

But that animal of my grandfather's isn't a horse. It's an old nag with a stiff neck.

I beg Uncle Neuch:

"Dear uncle, I want . . . I wish . . ."

"What?"

"To ride the old nag."

"But you don't know how, you couldn't."

"Oh yes I do."

The old nag is in front of me, head lowered.

She is sad. She mutters.

She smiles — at the grass, perhaps.

At last I mount her, I climb up on to her back without a saddle or anything, and, you know, her belly is huge.

My feet are wide apart, my arms are up in the air.

But the old nag is already off. I am carried away, tipped off on to the ground. I expect her hoofs to hit me.

But she races merrily off towards the fields, as fast as her legs will carry her.

We spend the whole evening looking for her.

Uncle scolds me. Where is that mare?

We shall find her far away in the forest, stumbling and tinkling her bell.

She is quietly munching the grass.

# 6

However, the years were passing by. It was time for me
to begin imitating others, to resemble them.

And one fine day, I saw before me a kind of tutor, a
little rabbi from Mohileff.

As though he had jumped out of my picture, or run
away from a circus.

He had not even been sent for. He came of his own
accord, the way the marriage-broker comes or the old
man who carries away corpses.

"A season or two..." he said to my mother.

How glib he is!

I look him straight in the face.

I already know that "a" with a line below it makes "o".
But at the "a" I fall asleep; at the line I would like to...
At that very moment the rabbi himself falls asleep.

How funny he is!

I would enter his class as promptly as a thunderbolt,
and I would come home every evening with a lantern in
my hand.

On Fridays he took me to the baths, making me lie down on a bench.

Birch twigs in hand, he would examine my body carefully, as if I were the Bible.

I had three such rabbis.

The first, a little bug from Mohileff.

The second, Rabbi Ohre (a nonentity, no memory of him).

The third, an imposing person who died early, Rabbi Djatkin.

He was the one who taught me that famous speech about "tefillin" which I recited standing on a chair when I reached the age of thirteen.

I confess, I felt duty bound to forget the man less than half an hour later, or even sooner.

I think my first little rabbi from Mohileff had the greatest influence on me.

Just imagine, every Saturday instead of going bathing in the river, my mother sent me to study the Bible with him.

However, I knew that at that time (immediately after lunch) the rabbi and his wife were sleeping soundly in honour of the Sabbath, completely undressed. Just wait until he gets into his trousers!

Once, knocking on the closed door, I attracted the attention of the lordly dog, a bad-tempered, red old beast with sharp fangs.

He padded softly down the stairs and, pricking up his ears, came towards me and . . .

I do not remember what happened next. I remember being picked up at the main entrance.

My arm bleeding, my leg too.

The dog had bitten me.

"Don't undress me, just put some ice on here . . ."

"We must carry him home to his mother as soon as possible."

That very day, that dog was hunted down by the police and it took them twelve shots to kill him.

That evening, I left for Petersburg for treatment, accompanied by my uncle.

The doctors declared I would die in four days.

Delightful! Everyone takes care of me. Every day brings me closer to death. I am a hero.

The dog was mad.

Going to Petersburg for treatment was very alluring.

I thought I might meet the Tzar in the street.

Passing the Neva, I had the impression that the bridge was hanging from the sky.

I forgot the dog-bite. It was a pleasure to sleep alone in a white bed, having yellow broth for lunch, with an egg.

It was a pleasure to stroll in the hospital garden; I thought I saw the Crown Prince among the well-dressed children playing there. I kept to myself, I did not play, I had no toys. I saw so many of them, such beautiful ones, for the first time.

They had never bought me any at home.

The uncle who had accompanied me advised me to take one of the abandoned toys quietly.

Adorable toy, it worried me far more than my angrily bitten arm.

But won't the little crown prince come and take it away from me?

The nurses smiled at me. Their smiles gave me confidence. But I always seemed to hear the sobs of the child who owned the stolen toy.

At last I recovered and left for home again.

I found the house full of finely dressed women and grave men, whose black shapes veiled the light of day.

A hullabaloo, whispering; suddenly, the piercing wail of a new-born child.

Mamma, half naked, is lying in bed – pale, with a faint pink flush. My younger brother had just been born.

Tables covered in white.

The rustle of holy vestments.

An old man, murmuring the prayer, cuts the little bit

of skin below the baby's stomach with a sharp knife . . .

He sucks the blood with his lips and smothers the baby's wails and cries in his beard.

I am sad. Silently, beside the others, I munch the cakes, herrings, gingerbread.

With every year that passed, I felt myself moving towards unknown horizons. Especially after the day when my father, wearing the tallit, muttered the prayer of expiation over my boyish thirteen-year-old body. What was I to do?

Remain an innocent child?

Pray morning and evening, everywhere I go, and say a prayer every time I put anything into my mouth or hear anything? Or flee the synagogue, throwing away the books, the holy vestments, and run through the streets towards the river?

I was afraid of my future coming of age, afraid of having all the signs of the adult man in my turn, even the beard.

In those sad, lonely days, these thoughts led me to weep towards evening, as though someone were beating me or announcing the death of my parents.

I looked into our vast, gloomy drawing room through the half-open door. There was nobody there. The looking glass, cold and solitary, swinging free, shone strangely.

I rarely looked at myself in it. I was afraid someone might catch me – in the act of admiring myself.

Long nose with – alas! – wide nostrils, shaped cheekbones, a rough profile.

At times I would stand lost in this contemplation.

What is the meaning of my youth?

I am growing in vain. Useless, short-lived beauty that congeals in the glass.

As soon as I reach thirteen, my carefree childhood will come to an end, and all the sins will fall on my head. Shall I sin?

I burst into loud laughter and splash the mirror with my white teeth.

One day my mother drags me to the elementary school. When I saw it from the outside I thought: "I'm sure to have a real stomach-ache here and the teacher won't let me go out."

But the cockade really is an attraction.

It will go on my cap, and if an officer goes by, won't I have to salute him?

Aren't we all equals – officials, soldiers, policemen and schoolboys?

But Jews are not accepted in this school.

Without hesitation, my brave mother approaches a teacher.

Our saviour, the only one we could get on with.

Fifty roubles is not much. I go straight into the third form, solely because that is his class.

With the school cap on my head, I began to study the open windows of the girls' school more boldly.

I wore a black uniform.

My body rebelled. And I certainly became sillier.

The teachers wear blue frock-coats, with gilt buttons.

How many thoughts crossed my mind as I gazed at them! How wise they were!

Where do they come from, what do they want?

I studied Nicolas Efimovitch's eyes, his back, and his blond beard.

I could not forget that he was the one who had accepted the bribe.

The other one, Nicolas Antonowitch, an impeccable scholar, would stride up and down the classroom, and although he read the reactionary newspapers, he was closer to me.

I did not always understand the kind of remarks he made to certain pupils.

After watching one boy for a long time, he would look him in the eyes and ask:

"Again, Volodia?"

Days went by before I discovered the meaning of that "again."

And why did they all blush except me?

In the next class I asked a friend to explain what Nicolas Antonowitch could be accusing Volodia of.

Smiling, he replied:

"Don't you know that Volodia mas . . . you fathead?"

All the same, it remained a mystery to me. The other boy laughed.

My God! My whole world was transformed and I was sad.

I don't know why, but at that time I began to stammer (on strike or something?).

Though I knew my lessons perfectly, I gave up reciting them. It was funny, but rather tragic.

To hell with noughts!

The sea of heads on all those benches completely bewildered me.

I began to tremble dreadfully, and when I went up to the board, I turned as black as soot and as red as a lobster.

Finished. Sometimes I even smiled.

That was the ecstasy of my stupefaction.

Naturally, it was useless when they prompted me from the front benches.

Yet I knew my lesson well. But I stammered.

I felt as if a red dog, like a bloodcurdling story, had bounded up and was baying over my prostrate body. My mouth was full of dust. My teeth were hardly white.

What was the good of those lessons?

I would have torn one hundred, two hundred, three hundred pages out of my books without caring, I would have thrown them to the winds.

Let them whisper all the words in the Russian language, the words of all countries and all seas, together to themselves in the air!

Let me alone!

I want to stay wild, cover myself with leaves, shout, weep, pray.

"Come, Chagall," says the teacher, "are you going to say your lessons today?"

I begin: "Ta . . . ta . . . ta . . ."

I thought they would throw me down from the fourth floor!

Life in uniform trembled like an autumn leaf.

But it all ended with me returning to my seat.

In the distance, the teacher's hand drew a very distinct "two."

I could still see that.

Through the classroom window I could see trees, the girls' school.

"Please may I leave the room, Nicolas Antonowitch?" I say, "I need to."

I had but one thought: "When will I have finished my lessons, will I have to go on with them much longer, and couldn't I leave without completing them?"

On days when we were not called to the board, when there was a general uproar in the class, I really didn't know what to do.

Stuck on my bench, pinched and prodded from all sides, I didn't know where to turn. I felt in my pockets for crusts of bread. I fidgeted, rocked backwards and forwards, stood up and sat down.

All of a sudden I put my head out of the window to blow a kiss to a sweet stranger.

The inspector comes towards me. He grabs my hand, holds it up.

Caught! I turn red, pink, pale.

"Remind me to give you a 'two' for conduct tomorrow, you wretch."

It was at this time that I began to revel in drawing. I did not know what that was to mean.

Sheets of drawings flew over the heads, often reaching the teacher's.

S . . . , the boy who sat next to me, indulged in his favourite pastime – thumping under the desk with his . . .

A muffled sound that sometimes attracted the teacher's attention.

Everyone fell quiet. Everyone laughed.

"Skorikoff!" shouts the teacher. He stands up, blushes, and after getting his "two" sits down again.

What I liked best was geometry.

At that, I was unbeatable. Lines, angles, triangles, squares, transported me into the realms of delight. And during the drawing period, I had everything but a throne.

I was the centre of the class, the object of its attention, and its example.

I only came to myself in the next lesson.

At the end of the year, after fencing with singlesticks and doing special exercises with the twenty-kilo weight, I had to stay down in the same class.

I don't remember what happened next.

Never mind! What's the use of hurrying?

I had plenty of time to become a clerk or an accountant. Let the time pass, let it drag!

Once again I'll sit up late at night with my hands in my pockets looking as if I'm working. Again I'll hear mother call from her room:

". . . You've burnt enough paraffin now! Go to bed. Didn't I tell you you ought to do your homework during the day? You're mad. Let me sleep!"

"But I'm not making any noise," I replied.

I look at the book, but I am thinking of the men who are walking down the streets at this moment, to my river, to the floating rafts bumping into the end of the bridge, sometimes smashing to pieces against it.

The planks split, springing up into the air, but the rowers escape.

Why don't they fall in too?

It would be interesting to see them perish like that.

I also think of the fat gentleman with puffy cheeks who

walks across the bridge, ogling the girls. In the café, he swallows half a dozen cakes at a time. He is fat, and thinks himself very intelligent.

In the library, he chooses the most serious newspapers. He reads them, puffing and blowing his nose with profuse apologies.

One day, at the tailor's, brandishing his cane, proud of his chubby youthfulness, he asks the tailor, his assistant, or even the boy:

"Excuse me sir, but please tell me – looking at me, how much cloth do you think I would need for a sensible pair of trousers?"

Fool, gas-bag, blockhead, idiot!

Listen what happened to me when I was in the fifth form, in the drawing lesson.

An old-timer in the front row, the one who pinched me the most often, suddenly showed me a sketch on tissue paper, copied from the magazine *Niwa*: The Smoker.

In this pandemonium! Leave me alone.

I don't remember very well, but this drawing, done not by me but by that fathead, immediately threw me into a rage.

It roused a hyena in me.

I ran to the library, grabbed that big volume of *Niwa* and began to copy the portrait of the composer, Rubinstein, fascinated by his crowsfeet and his wrinkles, or by a Greek woman and other illustrations; maybe I improvised some too.

I hung them all up in our bedroom.

I was familiar with all the street slang and the other, milder words that were current.

But a word as fantastic, as literary, as otherworldly as the word "artist" – well, I might have heard it, but it had never been uttered by anyone in our town.

It was so remote from us!

I would never have used the word of my own accord.

One day a friend called in, looked round our room and saw my drawings on the walls, and exclaimed:

"I say, so you're a real artist?"

"An artist, what's that? Who's an artist? Is it possible that I . . . too . . .?"

I immediately remembered that somewhere in our town I had actually seen a large sign, like a shop sign: "Penne the Painter's School of Painting and Design."

I thought: "The die is cast. I only have to join that school, and I'll become an artist."

And once and for all I shall shatter my mother's dreams of making me a clerk or an accountant or, even better, a well-established photographer.

# 7

One fine day (but all days are fine), while my mother
was putting the bread into the oven, I went up to her as
she held the scoop and, taking her by her floury elbow,
said:

"Mamma . . . I wish to be a painter.

"It's no good, I can't be a clerk or a book-keeper now.
I'm sick of that. It's not for nothing that I had a feeling
something was going to happen.

"Look, Mamma, am I a man like other men?

"What am I fit for?

"I wish to be a painter. Save me, Mamma. Come with
me. Come on, come on! There's a place in town; if I'm
admitted, and if I finish the course, I'll be a complete
artist by the time I leave. I should be so happy!"

"What? A painter? You're mad. Let me put my bread
in the oven; don't get in my way. My bread's there."

"Mother, I can't go on. Come!"

"Let me alone."

In the end, it is decided. We'll go to M. Penne's. And if

he sees that I have talent, then we shall think about it. But if not. . .

but on my own.)

(1 shall be a painter all the same, I thought to myself,

It's clear my fate is in M. Penne's hands, at least in the eyes of my mother, the head of the household. My father gave me five roubles, the monthly fee for the lessons, but he tossed them into the courtyard, and I had to run out for them.

I had discovered Penne from the platform of a tram that ran downhill towards Cathedral Square, when I was suddenly dazzled by a white inscription on a blue background: "Penne's School of Painting."

"Ah!" I thought, "what a clever town our Witebsk is!"

I immediately decided to make the acquaintance of the master.

That sign was actually only a big blue placard of sheet metal, exactly like the ones you can see on shop fronts everywhere.

As a matter of fact, small visiting cards and small door plates were useless in our town. No-one paid any attention to them.

"Gourevitch Bakery and Confectionery."

"Tobacco, All Brands."

"Fruit and Groceries."

"Warsaw Tailor."

"Paris Fashions."

"Penne the Painter's School of Painting and Design."

It's all business.

But the last sign seemed to come from another world.

Its blue is like the blue of the sky.

And it sways in the sun and the rain.

After rolling up my tattered sketches, I set out, trembling and anxious, for Penne's studio, accompanied by my mother.

Even as I climbed his stairs I was intoxicated, overwhelmed by the smell of the paints and the paintings.

Portraits on every side. The governor's wife. The governor of the town himself. Mr. L . . . and Mrs. L . . . , Baron K . . . with the Baroness, and many others. Did I know them?

A studio crammed with pictures from floor to ceiling. Stacks and rolls of paper are heaped on the floor too. Only the ceiling is clear.

On the ceiling, cobwebs and absolute freedom.

Here and there stand Greek plaster heads, arms, legs, ornaments, white objects, covered with dust.

I feel instinctively that this artist's method is not mine.

I don't know what mine is. I haven't time to think about it.

The vitality of the figures surprises me.

Is it possible?

As I climb the stairs I touch noses, cheeks.

The master is not at home.

I shall say nothing of my mother's expression and her feelings on finding herself in an artist's studio for the first time.

Her eyes darted into every corner, she glanced at the canvases two or three times.

Suddenly she swings round to me, and almost imploringly, but in a firm clear voice, she says:

"Well, my son . . . You can see for yourself; you'll never be able to do this kind of thing. Let's go home."

"Wait, Mamma!"

For my part, I have already decided that I will never do this kind of thing. Am I obliged to?

That's another question. But what? I don't know.

We wait for the master. He must decide my fate.

My God! If he's in a bad mood, he'll dismiss me with "That's no good."

(Everything is possible – be prepared, with or without Mamma!)

No-one in the studio. But someone is moving about in the other room. One of Penne's pupils, no doubt.

We go in. He hardly notices us.

"Good morning."

"Good morning, if you like."

He is sitting astride a chair, painting a study. I like that.

Mamma immediately asks him a question.

"Please tell me, Mr. S . . . What's this painting business like? Any good?"

"Ah well . . . it's not like shopkeeping or selling, to me."

Naturally, one couldn't expect a less cynical or less banal reply.

It was enough to convince my mother that she was right, and to instil a few drops of bitterness into me, stammering child.

But here is the dear master.

I would be lacking in talent if I could not describe him for you.

It does not matter that he is short. It only makes his profile more friendly.

The tails of his jacket hang in points down to his legs.

They float to the left, and to the right, up and down, and at the same time his watch-chain follows them.

His blond, pointed beard wags, expressing now melancholy, now a compliment, now a greeting.

We step forward. He bows casually. (One only bows carefully to the governor of the town and to the rich.)

"What can I do for you?"

"Well, I really don't know . . . he wants to be a painter . . . He must be mad! Please look at his drawings . . . If he has any talent, then it would be worth taking lessons, but otherwise . . . Let's go home, my son."

Penne did not bat an eyelid.

(You devil, I thought, give us a sign!)

He flicks mechanically through my copies of *Niwa* and mutters:

"Yes . . . he has some ability . . ."

Oh! You . . . I thought to myself in my turn.

My mother hardly understood any better, that's certain.

But for me, that was enough.

At all events, I got some five-rouble pieces from my father and took lessons for nearly two months in Penne's school in Witebsk.

What did I do there? I don't know.

A plaster model was hung up in front of me. I had to draw it at the same time as the others.

I set myself assiduously to this task.

I held the pencil up to my eyes, I measured and measured.

Never just right.

Voltaire's nose always hangs down.

Penne comes.

They sold paints in the shop next door. I had a box, and the tubes rolled about in it like children's corpses.

No money at all. For studies, I went to the far end of the town. The farther I went, the more frightened I grew.

Such was my fear of crossing the frontier and finding myself near military camps, that my colours became dingy, my painting turned sour.

Where are those studies on large canvases that hung above Mamma's bed: water-carriers, little houses, lanterns, processions on the hills?

It seems that because the canvas was coarse, they were put on the floor as carpets.

That's a fine thing!

We must wipe our feet. The floors have just been washed.

My sisters thought that pictures were painted for that very purpose, especially when they were done on large canvases.

I sighed, and almost decided to strangle myself.

In tears, I picked up my canvases and hung them once more at the door, but in the end they were taken up to the attic where, gradually covered with dust, they were peacefully buried for ever.

At Penne's, I was the only one to paint in violet. What's that?

Where does that idea come from?

It seemed so daring that from then on, I attended his school free of charge until, in the words of S . . . , it was no longer like shopkeeping or selling to me.

The outskirts of Witebsk. Penne.

The earth in which my parents sleep – all that is left of what was dearest to me.

I like Penne. I see his wavering silhouette.

He lives in my memory like my father. Often, when I think of the deserted streets of my town, he is in them, here or there.

More than once in front of his door, on the threshold of his house, I have longed to plead with him:

I don't want fame, I only want to be a silent craftsman like you; I would like to be hung like your paintings, in your street, near you, in your house. May I?

# 8

I have forgotten the name of those nights before holy days when the Jews make their way to the cemetery, one by one, or in groups.

After an hour or two, wormwood plants appear in the streets, like a naked body among clothed people.

I go there too, with my books. I arrive, and I sit down. I touch the hedges. Is that sad?

We two know how sweet it is to wander in such sleepy corners.

There, nothing remains alive, nothing stirs. Our feet brush against scraps of paper, notices, odd bits of letters, and those who wrote them are themselves lying somewhere here. At the foot of the graves, the grass is withering; footprints, damp and porous, disappear. The tomblike earth drinks the tears and each dead soul chokes and dies a second death. You must not weep on the graves. You must not lie down on the graves of children.

The memorial plate on the grave of my little sister Rachel disappeared long ago.

She wasted away as a result of eating charcoal. Finally, thin and pale, she breathed her last. Her eyes filled with heavenly blue, with dark silver. Her pupils froze. Flies swarmed down to her nose. No one brushed them away.

I rose from my chair, brushed them away, and sat down again. I got up again and sat down again.

Tears almost came to my eyes at the sight of the blazing candle at her head. An old man stood at her side, guarding her all night long.

And to think that in a few hours that little body will be put into the ground and men's feet will trample over it!

No-one gives a thought to dinner. My sisters have hidden behind the door-curtains; they weep, pressing their ten fingers to their mouths and wiping their tears away with their hair, with their blouses.

I couldn't understand how a living being can suddenly die.

I had often seen funerals, but I wanted to see the person who was in the coffin. I was afraid of it, too.

One morning, well before dawn, cries suddenly rose from the street, beneath the windows. In the feeble glow of the night-light, I managed to make out a woman running alone through the deserted streets.

She is waving her arms, sobbing, imploring the occupants, who are still asleep, to come and save her husband, as if I or the fat cousin dozing in her bed could cure, could save a dying man. She runs farther on.

She is afraid to stay alone with her husband.

Startled people come running from every side.

Everyone talks, gives advice, rubs his arms, his heaving chest.

They spray him with camphor, alcohol, vinegar.

Everyone groans, weeps.

But the steadiest, prepared for everything, push the woman aside, quietly light the candles and, in the midst of the silence, begin to pray aloud over the dying man's head.

The light of the yellow candles, the colour of that face, near-dead, the assured movements of the old men, their impassive eyes convince me, and those around me, that it is all over.

The rest of you can go back to your houses now, go back to bed again or light the samovar and open the shops.

All day long we shall hear the lamentations of the children singing the "Song of Songs".

The dead man is already lying on the ground in sad solemnity, his face illumined by six candles.

In the end, they carry him away.

Our street is no longer the same. I don't know it any more than I know those women who shriek wildly.

A black horse draws the coffin.

He is the only one to do simply his duty – he takes the dead man to the cemetery.


One day, a pupil of Penne's came to my house. The son of a big merchant, an old classmate of mine from the elementary school, which he had left for a more bourgeois school, a school of commerce. His peculiar merits resulted in the proposal that he should leave that one in turn.

Black hair, pale face, he was as much of a stranger to me as his family was to mine.

Whenever he met me on our bridge, he never failed to stop me and question me, blushingly, about the colour of the sky or the clouds, and asked me to give him lessons.

"Don't you think," he would say to me, "that that cloud over there, near the river, is intensely blue? When it is reflected in the water, it turns violet. You love violet like I do, don't you?"

I controlled the feelings that had been building up since my studies in that elementary school, where this aristocrat used to study me like an antique.

That boy had quite a pleasant face and I was often at a loss to know what to compare it with.

Ignoring the wealth and ease that surrounded him, he enriched my childhood years.

"All right," I said to him: "I'll be your teacher, but I won't take any money from you. Let's be friends instead."

I deserted the house more and more to spend all my days with him in his house in the country. Or we wandered over fields and meadows.

What is the point of writing all that? Because the distinction of my friends was the one thing that gave me a little courage to hope that I might ever be more than the humble boy from Pokrowskaja Street.

He had travelled and he told me he was preparing to leave for Petersburg, to continue his art studies there.

"I say, why don't we go together?"

What could I do, the son of a simple clerk? I had already been apprenticed to a photographer. He predicted a splendid future for me, provided I proved myself really punctual and agreed to work for him without pay for one more year.

"Art is a fine thing," he would say, "but it won't run away from you! And besides, what good is art? Consider my situation. Nice flat, fine furniture, customers, wife, children, respect; you'll have all that too. You'd better stay with me."

He was a well-to-do bourgeois, who took a pride in his appearance. How often I had the urge to scatter all his photographs and b . . . off!

I hated the retouching. I never mastered it. I did not see the point of blocking out those spots, wrinkles, and crowsfeet, of rejuvenating so many different faces, none of which were alive.

When I came across the picture of a girl friend, I smiled at her. I was ready to beautify that one!

I remember how my mother went to have her photograph taken for the first time.

There were medals on both sides of the photographer's sign. Imagine our excitement.

To get better value, our whole family, including the uncles and aunts, had decided to have themselves photographed together on one small card.

I, a little boy of five or six, dressed in a red velvet suit with gilt buttons, stood close to my mother's skirt. Like my sister, who was on the other side, I held my mouth open, so as to breathe better.

When we went to get the proofs, we bargained a bit, in the usual way.

The photographer lost his temper and tore the only copy of the photo to bits.

Stunned, I picked up the scattered pieces and stuck them together at home.

Thank God!

Another photographer I worked for was kinder. He groaned so loudly, you could hear him in the next room.

At least he paid me by feeding me. I shall never forget the soups, the large portions of meat they gave me and the other workers. And as much bread as I wanted.

Thank you!

Suddenly, something snaps.

Armed with my twenty-seven roubles, the only ones I ever received from my father in my life (for my art tuition) – I flee, still pink and curly-haired, to Petersburg, followed by my schoolmate. It is settled.

How tearfully and how proudly I picked up that money my father threw under the table (I forgive him, it was his way of giving). I bent down and picked it up.

On my knees under the table, I thought of the nights

of starvation ahead of me, alone in streets full of well-fed people.

But a little boy like me would want to eat, to have a roof over my head. There were moments when I thought it wouldn't be such a bad thing to stay there under the table, either.

In my answer to my father's questions, I stammered that I wanted to go to a school of a ... a ... a ... art.

I don't remember my father's reply or his grimace.

He immediately leapt up, as usual, to boil the samovar, and as he went, he flung at me:

"Well then, go if you like. But I want to tell you one thing – I have no money. You can see that for yourself. That's all I've scraped up. Impossible to send you anything. Don't count on it."

"It doesn't matter," I thought, "with or without money, I shall go.

"Is it possible that no-one, nowhere, will even give me a cup of tea? Is it possible I'll never find a piece of bread anywhere, on a bench or on a post?

"You often find that people leave a piece of bread behind, wrapped up in paper.

"The essential thing is art, painting, a painting different from the painting everyone else does.

"But what sort? Will God or someone give me the power to breathe my sigh into my canvases, the sigh of prayer and sadness, the prayer of salvation, of rebirth?"

Now, I remember, not a single day, not a single hour went by without me saying to myself, "I am still a boy."

No. Terror seized me; how would I manage to feed myself, being good for nothing except, perhaps, drawing?

But neither could I be a storeman like my father, for I hadn't the strength to lift huge barrels.

I was even glad that I had no choice but to become an artist. It was a good excuse for me not to have to earn my living. And certainly, I thought, being an artist, I shall become a man.

But in order to live in Petersburg, one needs not only money, but also a special permit. I am a Jew. And the Tzar has set aside a special zone of residence for the Jews, which they are not allowed to leave.

My father obtained a provisional certificate from a tradesman, as though I had been instructed to go and take delivery of some goods for him.

I set out (in 1907) towards a new life, in a new town.

# 9

Down at the docks I courted the girls. And in the timber yards, on the roofs, in the lofts, I enjoyed myself with my friends.

In front of our door, the noisy gossips of the house are sitting on a bench.

One of my schoolmates passes. I hide behind the door, poking my head out.

"Joseph, it's the exam tomorrow."

I shall spend the night at his house. I shall study his curly head.

"Let's do our homework together!"

Paykine and his toys, Jachnine and his herrings, Matzenko and his train all disturbed me a great deal.

But as long as I was enjoying myself in the courtyard, with a slice of bread and butter in my hands, peace reigned in our house.

All was quiet, too, when I was pursuing my studies at the elementary school, and accepting presents of ribbons from my little girl friends.

But the more I grew, the more frightened I became.

It appears that my father, having certain privileges in view for my elder brother, had added two years to my age on my birth certificate.

My early adolescence. Night. The house is asleep. The earthenware stove is hot. Father is snoring.

The street is asleep too, black and velvety.

Suddenly, someone outside – very close to the house – moves, blows his nose, whispers.

"Mamma!" I cried. "Surely it's the policeman coming to take me away to the regiment!"

"Hide under the bed quickly, son."

I creep underneath and stay there for a long time, quiet and happy.

You can't imagine how happy I am – and I don't know why – when I am lying down flat under a bed or on a roof in some sort of hiding place.

Under the bed – dust, shoes.

I plunge into my thoughts, I fly above the world.

But no policeman appeared. I leave my hiding place.

Then I am not a soldier? Still a little boy.

Thank heaven.

I get back into bed, and I dream of policemen, soldiers, epaulettes, and barracks.

Yet in the days when I was playing with sticks, walking over roofs during the great fires, bathing and drawing, nothing prevented me from persistently courting the girls down at the docks.

The sight of the high-school girls, the lace on their long drawers, their plaits, tormented me.

Must I admit that in the opinion of some people, and according to the evidence of the looking glass, my face in early adolescence was made up of a mixture of Passover wine, ivory-coloured flour, and rose-pink petals, strewn among the pages of a book?

How I admired myself, you will say!

My closest friends caught me more than once in front of the glass. As a matter of fact, I was studying myself and thinking of the difficulties I should have if I ever wanted to paint my portrait. But there was a touch of admiration in it – why not? I admit, I did not hesitate to blacken my eyes a little, to redden my mouth slightly, although it did not need it; and yes, yes . . . I did want to please the girls, down at the docks.

I was successful. But I have never been able to turn that success to my advantage.

Now I am at Lyozno with Nina. A promising walk. I feel it, and I tremble. Or quite the opposite.

We are under the bridge, beneath the roof of an old barn, on a bench.

Night. We are alone.

In the distance, a cab rumbles towards the station. No-one else about now. You can do what you want. And what do I want? I kiss her.

One kiss, two. Today, tomorrow, there will always be a limit.

Soon it is dawn. I am annoyed. We go to her parents' house. Inside, the air is stifling. Everyone is asleep.

Tomorrow is Saturday. And if they see me in the morning, they will all be glad of it.

A very suitable fiancée. They will congratulate both of us.

Shall I stay? What a night! How hot it is! Where are you? In fact, I know nothing of love in action. Hadn't I followed Aniouta for four years, sighing? And, at the end of the fourth year – with her encouragement – all I dared do was to give her one terrifying kiss one night outside the courtyard gate, just when her face was coming out in pimples.

A fortnight later, I was no longer speaking to her. What was the use? I had heard that an actor was taking her out.

How many scenes that violent girl staged in order to trap me!

How many private meetings were cunningly arranged by her and her friends!
courage had gone.

I can't think what was happening to me, or where my
As a man, I did not exist. She understood that, and I do know that it might all have taken quite a different turn if only I had been shrewder.

No, no.

I was scared stiff of her corset, which she wore on purpose.

I didn't understand a thing, and yet I did understand that I was wasting my time.

She used to go with me when I went out of town to paint on the Jules hill. It was futile. Neither the stillness of the nearby forest, nor the deserted valleys, nor the vast fields gave me the strength I would have needed to overcome my fear, and yet . . .

One evening I was sitting with her on the quay, at the end of the town, where the baths are.

Below, the river blends and flows gently.

"Try!" I thought.

My cap is on her head. I lean on her shoulder. That's all.

Suddenly I hear footsteps, a group of schoolmates are coming.

They're coming towards us, towards me. I want my cap back.

"Aniouta, give me back my cap," I say.

We leave the bench, but my cap is still on her head. They follow us.

Someone treats me to a violent blow in the back, then

runs away, shouting, "Leave her alone and don't you dare come down to this quay again, or else . . ."

I can no longer see you today, Aniouta.

It's a long time since that happened.

Now I am grown up; there is no childhood nor adolescence left in me, and so many sad thoughts in my head!

How I should like to bring those days back, to meet you again, to see your face, aged as it might be!

It used to be smooth, unwrinkled, and once or twice I ventured to kiss it. Do you remember?

You were the first to attract me and to kiss me. I stood speechless. My head was spinning. But I controlled myself, and I held the very same expression in my eyes, to show you how daring I was.

One day, you fell ill. You were lying in bed. There were little red spots on your face. I came up to you and sat down at the foot of the bed. I asked you if this was the result of the kiss I had given you the other night.

"No," you sighed, and you smiled.

That time will never return.

On the skating rink, under the bridge, I met your friend Olga, a high-school girl. A square face, rather a snub nose, a slight squint.

When I saw her, I felt the pangs of a woman with child. Desires of all kinds seethed up in me, but she dreamt of eternal love.

I wanted to hide somewhere and make her vanish from the face of the earth.

But I pitied her for her thin hands and her rather short legs.

When I gave her up I sent her some farewell verses, saying that I was not made for the eternal love that she dreamt of.

With my third romance I grew bolder. I kissed left and right. I didn't try to stop myself any more.

Is it worth boring you and boring myself by recounting my childish romances?

Year after year, the nights faded out above me and, behind the fences, love died in vain the very moment it was born.

In the gardens and avenues, those kisses on the benches have long since withered.

The rains have washed them away.

Now no-one speaks your names.

I shall walk past your streets, and I shall transfer the bitterness of desolate meetings to my canvases.

Let the mists of our days shine there, there let them fade.

And the stranger who sees them will smile.


I am at Thea's, lying on the couch in the consulting room of her father, the doctor. I liked to stretch out like that near the window, on that couch covered with a worn black oil-cloth, with holes in several places.

This must have been the very couch on which pregnant women were examined, and people who were sick in the stomach, the head, or the heart.

I lay down on that couch, my head on my arms, and, dreaming, I studied the ceiling, the door, the place where Thea usually sat.

I am waiting for her. She's busy. She is preparing the dinner – fish, bread and butter – and her great big dog is circling round her legs.

I lay down there deliberately, so that Thea would come near me, so that she would kiss me. I held out my arms, the arms of salvation.

The bell rings. Who is it?

If it's her father coming home, I shall have to get up and go away.

Who is it then?

It's one of Thea's friends. She comes in. Her voice rings out, she chatters to Thea.

I stay in the consulting room. I don't go out. Yes, I did

go out, but the friend had her back to me and couldn't see me.

I feel . . . What do I feel?

On the one hand, I am annoyed that someone has disturbed my rest, my hope that Thea might come to me.

On the other hand, that stranger's visit, and her singing voice, disturbs me, as if it were from another world.

Who is she? I am afraid. No, I want to face her, to be near her.

But she is already saying goodbye to Thea. She hardly looks at me, and goes away.

Thea and I go out for a walk. On the bridge we meet her again.

She is alone, all alone.

Suddenly I feel that I should not be with Thea, but with her!

Her silence is mine. Her eyes, mine. It's as if she had known me for a long time, and knew all my childhood, my present, and my future; as if she had been watching over me, reading my inmost thoughts, although I have never seen her before.

I knew that this was she — my wife.

Her pale face, her eyes. How big, round and black they are! They are my eyes, my soul.

I saw that Thea was nothing to me — a stranger.

I have entered a new home, and I am not to be parted from it.

# 10

The room at Javitch's, in our courtyard, was my studio. To reach it, you had to pass through the kitchen, the owner's dining room, where that tall, bearded old man, a leather merchant, sat at the table and drank his tea.

When I passed through his room, he would turn his head slightly: "Good day."

But I felt embarrassed when I saw the lamp on the table and two plates, from which protruded an enormous bone.

His daughter, an ugly brunette, the perennial fiancée, smiled a strange, broad smile. Her hair was like an icon's, and her eyes shifted timidly.

When she saw me, she covered herself desperately with a scarf or a cloth.

My room was lit by the deep blue that fell through the only window. The light came from a distance: from the hill, where the church stood.

I always enjoy painting that church and that little hill again in my pictures.

I often jumped into bed, feet in the air. Canvases on the walls, blurred windows, dust, a solitary chair and flimsy table.

Bella knocks at the door, knocks timidly with her thin, slender little finger.

In her arms, clutched to her breast, she holds a big bunch of mountain ash, cloudy green splashed with red.

"Thank you," I say, "thank you."

That wasn't the right word.

It's dark. I kiss her.

A still life magically takes shape in my mind.

She poses for me.

Reclining, a rounded white nude takes shape.

I approach her timidly. I confess it was the first time I had seen a nude.

Although she was practically my fiancée I was still afraid of approaching her, of going any nearer, of touching all that loveliness.

As if a feast were spread before your eyes.

I did a study of her and hung it on the wall.

The next day my mother comes into my room and sees the study.

"What's that?"

A naked woman, the breasts, the dark patches.

I am embarrassed; so is she.

"Take that girl down!" she says.

"Little Mamma! I love you very much. But . . . have you never seen yourself in the nude? I look, and all I do is sketch her. That's all."

But I obeyed my mother. I took the canvas down and I did another picture to replace the nude – a procession.

Soon I moved into another room, in a policeman's house.

I was very pleased with it. I felt he was guarding me day and night.

You can paint whatever you like.

Bella can come and go as she wishes.

The policeman was a tall man with a drooping moustache — just like the pictures.

In front of his house stood the Ilyinsky church. It was snowing.

One night, when I went out with Bella to take her back to her parents' house, our feet struck a large bundle, while we were kissing.

"What's that?"

An abandoned baby. A frail mite, swathed in dark wool, whimpering.

Proudly I hand it over to my powerful policeman.

Another time, it is already dark, Bella can't get out; the door is locked.

The little lamp is smoking. The fire irons stand sleepily in front of the kitchen stove. Everything is stock still. A few empty saucepans lie about.

How can I get her out? What will the sleeping neighbours think?

"Look," I say to her, "get through the window!"

That makes us laugh. I let her down through the window into the alley.

The next day, people whispered in the courtyard and in the street: "You know, she even climbs through the window to get in and out of his room. It's gone that far!"

Just try and tell them my fiancée is purer than Raphael's Madonna and I'm an angel!

As many rooms and alcoves to rent as you want. The advertisements are as common as the damp. On my arrival in Petersburg, I had rented a room that I shared with a

budding sculptor, whom the writer Sholem Aleichem described as a future Antokolsky (he was soon to become a doctor).

He howled like a wild beast and flung himself furiously on his clay to keep it from drying out.

Is that any of my business?

All the same, I'm a man. I can't wake up every time he sniffs.

One day I threw the lamp at his head and said to him: "Clear out, go to your Sholem Aleichem; I want to be alone."

As soon as I arrived in the capital I went to take the entrance examination for Baron Steglitz's School of Arts and Crafts.

"This is the place," I thought as I looked at the building, "where one gets permission to live in the capital, and a grant to live on."

But everything alarmed me – the studies, and copying those long plaster decorations that looked like things in a shop.

I thought: These decorations were deliberately chosen to frighten you, to put the Jewish students off and prevent them getting the vital permit.

Alas! My suspicion was right.

I failed the examination. I got no recommendation and no grant. Nothing could be done about it.

I had to enrol in an easier school, the one run by the Society for the Protection of the Arts, where I went straight into the third year without an examination.

What did I do there? I couldn't tell you.

Numerous plaster heads of Greek and Roman citizens projected from every corner and I, poor provincial, had to pore over the wretched nostrils of Alexander of Macedon – or some other plaster idiot.

Sometimes I walked up to those noses and punched them. And, from the back of the room, I stood and stared at the dusty breasts of Venus.

81

Although they approved of my style of painting, I saw no results.

I couldn't keep cool when I saw those cab-driver students digging into the paper with their rubber and sweating, as if they were using a shovel.

They were not bad fellows at heart. My Semitic appearance aroused their curiosity. They even advised me to collect all my sketches (I haven't kept a single one) and enter them in the competition.

When I found I was one of the four selected for a scholarship, I had the feeling that the past was behind me for ever.

I drew ten roubles a month for a whole year.

I was rich and I treated myself to a meal in a little restaurant in Zoukowskaja Street almost every day – after which, as a rule, I nearly passed out.

Guinzbourg the sculptor came to my rescue.

Skinny, short, with a black beard, an excellent man. I remember him with particular gratitude.

His studio, in the Academy of Fine Arts itself, filled with souvenirs of his master Antokolsky and his own busts of all the contemporary celebrities, seemed to me to be a centre inhabited by the elect who had travelled life's hard road.

In fact, that little man was in close contact with Leo Tolstoy, Stassoff, Repin, Gorki, Chaliapin, etc. He was at the height of his fame whereas I – I was a nonentity, without any right to live, without the smallest monthly income.

I don't know whether he found any particular virtues in my adolescent studies.

In any case, he provided me, in his usual way, with a letter of recommendation to Baron David Guinzbourg.

The latter, who saw a future Antokolsky in every boy who was sent to him (how many shattered illusions!) made me a monthly allowance of ten roubles, for a few months only.

And after that, you're on your own!

That erudite Baron, an intimate friend of Stassoff, knew next to nothing about art.

But he thought it his duty to engage me in elegant conversation, telling me stories followed by a moral, to show that an artist should be very careful.

"Take Antokolsky's wife, for instance, she was no good. It seems she drove beggars away from her door. Beware of that! Be careful! ... A wife can be very important in an artist's life."

I was thinking of something else, with respect.

I drew his allowance for four or five months.

I thought: "The Baron receives me nicely enough, he talks to me. Why shouldn't he provide for my needs, so that I can live and work?"

One day when I went to collect the ten roubles, his magnificent man-servant said, as he handed them to me:

"Here you are, and it's the last time."

Had the Baron and his whole family considered what would become of me when I left his palatial stairs? Could I, at seventeen, manage to earn a living with my sketches – or did he simply think: "Look out for yourself, go and sell newspapers."

Then why had he done me the favour of talking to me as if he had faith in my artistic ability?

I couldn't understand it. And there was nothing to understand.

I was the one who suffered, no-one else. I hadn't even a place where I could draw.

Goodbye, Baron!

At that time I was introduced to a galaxy of rich patrons. Everywhere in their drawing rooms I always felt red-faced and hot, as if I had just come out of the bath.

Oh for a permit to live in the capital!

Now I am a servant in lawyer Goldberg's house.

Lawyers have the right to keep Jewish servants.

But, according to the law, I must live in his house and have my meals there.

We became great friends.

In the spring, he took me to their estate at Narwa, where his wife and her sisters, the Germontes, radiated so much affection – in the vast rooms, in the shade of the trees, and on the seashore.

Dear Goldbergs! You are before my eyes!

But before I met those good patrons, I didn't know where to lay my head.

My means did not permit me to rent a room; I had to make do with alcoves. I didn't even have a bed all to myself. I had to share it with a workman. It's true he was an angel, that workman with the dark black moustache.

He was so kind to me that he flattened himself right up against the wall in order to give me more room. With my back to him, and my face to the window, I breathed in the fresh air.

In those communal alcoves, with workmen and barrow-boys for neighbours, there was nothing for me to do but lie down on the edge of my bed and consider myself. What else? And dreams oppressed me: A square, empty room. In one corner, a single bed, and me on it. It is getting dark.

Suddenly, the ceiling opens and a winged being descends with a crash, filling the room with movement and clouds.

A rustle of trailing wings.

I think: An angel! I cannot open my eyes, it's too light, too bright.

After rummaging about all over the place, he rises and passes through the opening in the ceiling, taking all the light and the blue air away with him.

Once again it is dark. I wake up.

My picture "The Apparition" evokes this dream.

Another time I rented half a little room somewhere in Panteleïmonowsky Street. At night, I couldn't understand where all the noise, that kept me from sleeping, came from.

The other half of the room was separated from mine only by a curtain. Why those snores?

Another time, the tenant in the other half of the room, a drunkard, a printer in the day, and an accordionist in the public gardens in the evening, came in late at night and, after stuffing himself with pickled cabbage, insisted on having his wife.

She pushed him away, took refuge in my half of the room, then ran off down the corridor, clad only in her nightgown. He pursued her, knife in hand.

"How dare you refuse me, your lawful husband?"

I realized then that in Russia, it is not only the Jews who have no right to live, but also a great many Russians, crowded together like lice in the hair. My God!

I moved again.

My room-mate was a Persian, of rather mysterious origin. He had fled his country, where he had been at one time a revolutionary, at another, attached to the suite of the former Shah. One wasn't very sure.

He loved me as if I were a bird, dreaming all the time of his Persia or of his mysterious affairs.

Later, I learnt that this former follower of the Shah had committed suicide on the streets of Paris.

Meanwhile, my trials were being renewed for lack of that famous permit, and also because my military service was drawing near.

One day, returning to Petersburg after the holidays, without a pass, I was arrested by the Commissioner himself.

The official who issued passports, not having received the expected tip (I hadn't understood) insulted me violently and ordered:

"Hey, here! Arrest him . . he entered the capital without a permit! Shove him in the lock-up with the thieves, for now; you can have him taken to prison later."

It was done.

Thank God! At last I am in peace.

Here, at least, I have the right to live. Here I can have quiet, plenty of food, and perhaps I'll even be able to draw in peace!

Nowhere else had I felt so relaxed as in that cell, where they took off all my clothes and made me put on prison uniform.

The slang of the thieves and prostitutes was very entertaining. They did not insult me or knock me about. I even had their respect.

Later I was transferred to a separate cell with an eccentric old man.

I enjoyed barging into that long lavatory again and again, without any need, deciphering the scribbles that plastered the walls and doors, lingering at the long table in the refectory over a bowl of water.

And, in that double cell, when the electricity unfailingly went off about nine o'clock at night, so that I couldn't go on reading or drawing, I slept soundly. The dreams started again.

Here is one of them: Several children of the same father – I am one of them – are on the seashore somewhere.

All of them, except me, are locked up in a wild animal's cage, a high, wide one. The father, an orang-outang with a tawny muzzle, holds a whip in his hand; now he threatens us, now he groans.

Suddenly, we have the urge to go and bathe like my elder brother Wrubel, the Russian painter, who also appeared as one of my brothers, I don't know why.

The first one they brought out was Wrubel.

I remember watching our favourite undressing. We see his golden legs in the distance, opening like scissors. He swims out towards the open sea. But the unbridled sea roars and boils. A cloud of angry waves rears up, like high ridges. The waves, as thick as molasses, thunder as they roll. What has become of my poor brother? We are all worried. All we can see in the distance is his little head – his legs no longer gleam.

At last, even the head disappears.

An arm is thrust out of the water, and then nothing more.

86

All the children screamed:

"He's drowned! Our eldest brother Wrubel's drowned!"

Father repeated in his deep voice:

"He's drowned, our son Wrubel. We only have one painter left, you, my son."

So it was I.

I woke up.

Released at last, I decided to learn a trade of some kind that would give me the right to a permit to live in the capital. So I became apprenticed to a sign-painter in order to get a certificate from a professional school.

I dreaded the examination. I might be able to draw fruit or a Turk smoking, but I was sure to fail on the lettering. However, I took a passionate interest in signs and I did a whole series of them.

It was good to see my first signs swinging in the market outside a butcher's or a greengrocer's, with a pig or a hen fondly scratching itself nearby, while the wind and the rain heedlessly spattered them with mud.

## II

But however closely I attended the course at the School
for the Protection of the Arts, I had the feeling I should
never be satisfied with it.

The teaching was non-existent. Our director, Roehrich,
wrote unreadable poems, books on history and archaeology,
and smiling through clenched teeth read parts of them
out loud, I don't know why – even to me, a pupil in his
school, as if I might have understood something of them.

Two years wasted in that school. It was cold in the class-
rooms. The smell of damp combined with the smell of
clay, paints, pickled cabbage and stagnant water in the
Moyky Canal; so many smells, real or imaginary.

Although I make an effort to work, all I have is a feeling
of bitterness. Yet I hear nothing but praise all around me.
I realize there is no sense in going on like this.

From time to time, my long-legged teacher in the still-
life class rebukes me in front of the whole room.

It's true, his pupils' daubs particularly infuriated me. They spent several years in the same class.

I didn't know what to do, or how to do it. Whether to rub charcoal and fingers over the paper or yawn like the others.

In the eyes of my teacher, my studies were meaningless daubs.

After hearing criticisms like: "What rubbish is that you've drawn?" and "a scholarship holder, too!" I left the school for good.

At that time, Bakst's school in school in Petersburg was beginning to make its name.

As far from the Academy as it was from the School for the Protection of the Arts, it was the only school animated by a breath of Europe. But the thirty roubles a month alarmed me. Where could I get them?

M. Sew, who always smiled and said: "Drawing, drawing first and foremost, think about that!" gave me a letter of recommendation to M. Bakst.

Summoning up all my courage, I collected my sketches, the ones I had done in class and the others I had painted at home, and took them to Bakst's house in Serguiewskaïa Street.

"The master's still asleep," answered Léon Bakst's mysterious maid.

One o'clock in the afternoon and still in bed, I thought.

Silence. No children's shouts, no woman's perfume. On the walls, pictures of Greek gods, a black velvet altar curtain from a synagogue, embroidered with silver. Strange. As I once stammered to M. Penne: "My name is Marc, I have a very delicate stomach and no money, but they say I have talent," so I whisper timidly in Bakst's anteroom.

He's still asleep, but he'll come soon. I must think what to say to him.

That's it, I know what I'll say to him, I can feel it already: "My father is a mere storeman, and your apartment is very clean. . ."

I've never before been so upset having to wait.

Here he is at last. I haven't forgotten the smile, tinged with pity or perhaps kindness, with which he greeted me.

It seemed to me that it was pure chance that he was wearing European clothes. He is a Jew. Reddish curls clustered above his ears. He could have been my uncle, my brother.

I began to think that he was born not far from my ghetto, and that he had also been a pink and white boy like me; perhaps he even stammered like me.

Entering Bakst's school, seeing him, upset me, I don't know why.

Bakst. Europe. Paris.

He'll understand me; he'll understand why I stammer, why I am pale, why I'm so often sad and even why I paint in lilac colours.

He stood before me, half smiling, and showing a row of shining pink and gold teeth.

"What can I do for you?" he said.

On his lips certain words drawled in an unusual way, and this particular accent made him seem more European than ever.

His fame, after the Russian season abroad, turned my head, I don't know why.

"Let me see your studies," he said.

What . . . me . . . Not a chance of backing out or acting shy. If my first visit to Penne only mattered to my mother, the one I paid Bakst mattered a great deal to me, and his opinion (whatever it was) would be decisive.

I only asked one thing; that there should be no mistake. Would he think I had talent, yes or no?

Looking through my studies, which I picked up one by one from the floor where I had piled them, he drawled in his lordly accent:

"Ye . . . es, ye . . . es, there's talent there; but you've been spoi . . . led, you're on the wrong track, spoi . . . led."

Enough! My God, me? The scholarship holder at the

School for the Protection of the Arts, on whom the director mechanically lavished his flashing smiles, whose style (damn it) was praised, but who was never sure of himself, took no satisfaction at all in his own daubs.

But Bakst's voice, his words – "spoiled, but not completely" – saved me.

Had anyone else said it, I should have taken no notice at all. But Bakst's authority is too great for me to dismiss his opinion. I stand and listen to him in awe, believing every word, while I awkwardly roll my canvases and my sketches.

I shall never forget that meeting with Bakst.

What is the use of pretending: something in his art would always be alien to me.

Perhaps the fault did not lie in him, but in the artistic society *Mir Iskoustva,* to which he belonged, where stylization, aestheticism and all kinds of worldly styles and mannerisms flourished; for this society, the revolutionaries of contemporary art – Cézanne, Manet, Monet, Matisse and the others – were no more than initiators of passing fashions.

Wasn't this the case with the famous Russian critic Stassoff who, dazzled and blinded by his national and ethnological prophecies, then so fashionable, led so many of his contemporaries astray? Without even knowing there was such a place as Paris, I found a miniature Europe in Bakst's school.

Bakst's pupils, all more or less gifted, at least knew where they were going. I became more and more convinced that I must forget all about my past.

I set to work. A model was posing, fat pink legs, a blue background.

In the studio, among the pupils, were Countess Tolstoy and the dancer Nijinsky.

I am overawed again.

I had heard it said that Nijinsky was already a famous dancer and that he had been dismissed from the Imperial Theatre solely on account of his daring costumes.

His easel stands next to mine. He draws rather clumsily like a child.

When he came up, Bakst simply smiled, patting him on the shoulder.

Nijinsky smiled at me too, as if to encourage me in my boldness, of which I was not yet aware. That brought us closer together.

The study is finished. Bakst corrects on Fridays.

He only comes in once a week. Then all the pupils stop work. The easels are lined up. We are waiting for him. Here he is.

He goes from one canvas to another, not knowing exactly whose they are.

He only asks: "Whose is this?" afterwards. He says little – one or two words – but hypnosis, fear, and the breath of Europe do the rest.

He is coming towards me. I am lost. He talks to me; more precisely, he talks about my study without knowing (or pretending not to know) that it's mine. He makes a few casual remarks, the way people do in polite conversation.

All the pupils look at me pityingly.

"Whose study is this?" he finally asks.

"Mine."

"I wondered. Naturally," he adds.

In an instant the memory of all my alcoves, all my poor rooms, flashed across my mind, but I had never felt so uncomfortable anywhere as I did after that remark of Bakst's.

I felt that things couldn't go on like this.

I did another study. Friday. Bakst arrives. No praise.

I fled from the studio. For three months, Allia Berson, who was understanding and kind to me, paid for the lessons uselessly, while I was absent.

It was more than I could handle. The fact is, I'm not capable of learning. Or rather, I can't be taught. I told you I was a bad pupil in elementary school. I grasp nothing except by instinct. Do you understand? and scholastic theory has no hold on me.

In short, my going to school had been more a matter of getting information, of communicating, than of being taught in the proper sense of the word.

After the fiasco of my first two studies in Bakst's school, for reasons I didn't understand, I fled in order to find my bearings in freedom and to try and shake off the yoke that encumbered me.

I only returned to school three months later, determined not to give in and to win the master's approval in front of all those distinguished pupils.

I forgot everything I had been taught, and I did a new study.

The following Friday it was judged by Bakst and hung on the studio wall as a sign of distinction.

It was not long before I realized there was nothing more for me in that school. Especially as Bakst himself, following the latest Russian season abroad, was leaving the school, and Petersburg too, for good.

I stammer:

"Léon Samuëlewitch, could you . . .? You know, Léon Samuëlewitch, I would like to . . . go to Paris."

"Ah! If you like. Tell me, can you paint scenery?"

"Certainly." (I hadn't the faintest idea).

"Here's a hundred francs then. Learn the job properly, and I'll take you."

Well, our ways parted, and I left for Paris all on my own.

I urged my father to rebel.

"Father," I told him, "listen; you already have a grown-up son, a painter. When will you give up making a fortune for your boss with that infernal work of yours? Look, didn't I faint often enough in Petersburg? Haven't I eaten enough minced cutlets? What will become of me in Paris?"

And he replied:

"What, me go away? And you support me? I can see that!"

My mother put a brave face on it.

"My son, we are your parents. Write to us more often. Ask us for anything."

My native earth gave way beneath my feet. The harsh river flowed furiously; it was not the river on whose banks I kissed you . . .

The Ouspene church, on top of the hill, the dome above it. The Dwina seems farther and farther away. I am no longer a boy.


As soon as I first learned how to express myself in Russian, I started to write verses. It came just as naturally as breathing.

What's the difference between a word and a sigh? I used to read them aloud to my friends. They wrote poems too, but as soon as I read them mine, their poetry vanished.

I suspected V . . . of passing off translations of foreign poems as his own work.

I longed to show my verses to a real poet, one of those who have their poetry published.

I ventured to ask Guinzbourg, the sculptor, to show them to a poet who was one of his friends, and was enjoying a certain popularity at the time.

But as soon as I mentioned this desire (and how agonizing it was even to open my mouth), he began to pace up and down his studio, pushing his way through his statues, and shouting:

"What? Why? What for? A painter doesn't want that. There's no need! It musn't be allowed. There's no need!"

I was startled, but calmed at the same time.

There really is no need.

Later, when I met Alexander Blok, a poet of rare and subtle talent, I again had the urge to show him my verses and ask his opinion.

But his eyes and his face halted me, like a vision of nature.

And I threw out, abandoned, or lost the only book of my juvenile poems.

Everyone is at home. In Petrograd, the Duma is sitting. The *Retz* newspaper. The atmosphere is electric.

And I paint my pictures. Mamma supervises my painting. She thinks, for instance, that in the picture "Birth" the stomach of the confined woman should be bandaged.

I satisfy her wish immediately.

It was right; the body comes to life.

Bella brings me some blue flowers, mixed with foliage. She is all in white, with black gloves. I paint her portrait.

Once I have counted all the hedges in the village, I paint "Death".

Once I've taken the pulse of all my family and friends, I paint "The Wedding".

But I felt that if I stayed in Witebsk any longer, I should be covered with hair and moss.

I roamed the streets, I searched and prayed.

"God, Thou who hidest in the clouds, or behind the cobbler's house, lay bare my soul, the aching soul of a stammering boy, show me my way. I do not want to be like all the others; I want to see a new world."

In answer, the town seems to snap like the strings of a violin, and all the inhabitants begin walking above the earth, leaving their usual places. Familiar figures install themselves on the roofs and settle down there.

All the colours spill out, dissolve into wine, and liquor gushes out of my canvases.

I am very happy with all of you. But . . . have you heard of traditions, of Aix, of the painter with severed ear, of cubes, of squares, of Paris?

Witebsk, I'm forsaking you.

Stay on your own with your herrings!

I confess, I couldn't say that Paris had any great attraction for me.

Nor did I feel any elation when I left Witebsk for Petersburg.

I knew that I had to leave. I found it difficult to define exactly what I wanted.

Too provincial, if I must admit it frankly.

Although I liked travelling, all I dreamt of was of being alone in a cage.

I often said that I would have been forever satisfied with a little room, with a grating in the door through which someone could pass me my food.

It was in that spirit that I went to Petersburg and, later, to Paris, But I didn't have enough money to make the journey to Paris.

If I were not to be lost among the thirty thousand artists who had come to Paris from every land and every nation, I must, first of all, find a means of living and working there.

At this time I was introduced to M. Vinaver, an eminent member of the Duma.

Don't imagine that only political or social celebrities could approach him.

I can say today, with deep sorrow, that in him I lost a man who was very close to me, almost a father.

I remember his sparkling eyes, the way his eyebrows moved slowly up and down, the sensitive line of his mouth, his light brown beard, the whole noble profile that I – still timid, alas! – never dared paint.

In spite of the difference between him and my father, who did nothing but go to the synagogue, while M. Vinaver was elected by the people, they were rather alike, all the same.

Were it not for him, I might have remained a photographer, established myself in Witebsk, and never had any idea of Paris.

During my stay in Petersburg, I had no permit to live

there, nor the smallest place to live in: no bed, no money.

More than once, I looked enviously at the oil lamp burning on the table.

Look how comfortably it burns away there on the table in the room, I thought. It drinks as much oil as it likes, and look at me!

I'm hardly sitting on the chair, on the edge of the chair. And the chair isn't mine. The chair without a room.

I daren't even sit down quietly. I'm hungry. I dream about the parcel of sausages a friend of mine received.

In general, I've been seeing bread and sausages in my dreams for years.

And, on top of that, an urge to paint.

Somewhere over there, rabbis in green are sitting waiting for me, peasants in their baths, red Jews, kind and intelligent, their sticks, their sacks, in the streets, in the houses, and even on the roofs.

They wait for me, I wait for them, we wait for each other.

But, on the other hand, the streets are watched by policemen at the police station, porters at the doors, "passportists" at the commissariats.

As I wandered through the streets, I read the menus at restaurant doors as if they were poems – the specialities of the day and the price of each dish.

Then Vinaver put me up not far from his house, in Zacharjewskaja Street, in the flat occupied by the editorial staff of the magazine *Dawn*.

I copied a painting he owned by Levitan. I liked the moonlight in it. As though candles were shining behind the canvas.

I didn't dare have the picture taken down from the wall where it had been hung, very high up, and I copied it standing on a chair.

I took the copy to a picture-framer who also made enlargements.

To my great surprise, he paid me ten roubles.

When I passed the shop a few days later, I saw my copy, prominently displayed in the window and bearing the signature "Levitan". The proprietor smiled sweetly and asked me to do some more for him.

A little later, I took him a pile of my own canvases. Perhaps he'll sell a few of them, I thought.

But the next day, when I went in to ask him if he had sold anything, he replied with an air of astonishment: "Pardon me, sir, but who are you? I don't know you."

In this way I lost about fifty of of my canvases.

Vinaver did everything to encourage me.

Like M. Syrkine and M. Sew, he dreamt of seeing me become a second Antokolsky.

Every day, as he climbed the stairs to his apartment, he would smile at me and ask:

"Well! How's it going?"

The editorial office was full of my canvases and drawings. It didn't look anything like an editorial office now, more like a studio. My thoughts on art mingled with the voices of the editors who came to confer and to work.

In the intervals, and at the end of the meeting, they crossed my "studio" and I hid behind the stacked copies of *Dawn* that occupied half the room.

Vinaver was the first person in my life to buy two of my pictures.

Although he's a lawyer and a well-known member of the Duma, he still likes those poor Jews coming down with the bride, the bridegroom, and the musicians from the top of my canvas.

One day, he runs into the editorial-studio panting, and says: "Get your best canvases together quickly and come up to my apartment. A collector saw your pictures at my house; he's very interested in them."

Flustered at seeing Vinaver himself come to my room, I couldn't find anything good.

Once, on Easter Day, Vinaver had invited me to his house for dinner.

The room shone with the reflection of the blazing candles, their odour blending with the dark ochres of Vinaver's complexion.

His wife, smiling as she gave orders, looked as though she had stepped out of a fresco by Veronese.

The table gleamed, awaiting the prophet Elijah.

And later, Vinaver always came in to see me again, and asked, with a smile: "Well! How's it going?"

I daren't show him my pictures in case he doesn't like them. He often said that he was an outsider in art.

But outsiders are my favourite critics.

In 1910, after choosing two pictures, Vinaver guaranteed me a monthly allowance that enabled me to live in Paris.

I set off.

Four days later, I arrived in Paris.

## 12

Only the great distance that separates Paris from my native town prevented me from going back home immediately or at least after a week, or a month.

I even wanted to invent a holiday of some kind, just as an excuse to go home.

It was the Louvre that put an end to all this wavering.

When I walked round the Veronese room and the rooms where the Manets, Delacroix, and Courbets are, I wanted nothing more.

In my imagination, Russia took the form of a paper balloon hanging from a parachute. The deflated bulb of the balloon sagged, cooled off, and collapsed slowly as the years went by.

That's how Russian art appeared to me, or something like it.

Indeed, whenever I happened to think about Russian art or talk about it, I had the same disturbing, mixed feelings, full of bitterness and resentment.

It was as if Russian art had been condemned by fate to follow in the wake of the West.

If Russian painters were condemned to be the pupils of the West, they were, I think, rather wayward pupils, by their very nature. The best Russian realist shocks when compared with the realism of Courbet.

The most authenic Russian impressionism is puzzling when it is compared with Monet and Pissarro.

Here, in the Louvre, before the canvases of Manet, Millet, and others, I understood why my alliance with Russia and Russian art had not worked. Why my very language is foreign to them.

Why no-one has faith in me. Why the artistic circles ignore me.

Why, in Russia, I'm only the fifth wheel of the coach.

And why everything I do seems outlandish to them, and everything they do seems futile to me.

I can say no more.

I love Russia.


In Paris, I thought I had found everything, particularly the skills of the craft.

I saw proof of it everywhere, in the museums and in the exhibitions.

Perhaps the East had got lost in my soul; or perhaps the dog-bite had reacted on my mind.

But it was not only within the profession that I looked for the meaning of art.

It was as though the gods stood before me.

I no longer cared to think of the neo-classicism of David or Ingres, the romanticism of Delacroix, and the reconstruction of early drawings of the followers of Cézanne and Cubism.

I had the feeling we are still only skimming over the surface of matter, that we are afraid of plunging into chaos, of breaking up the familiar ground under our feet and turning it over.

The very first day after my arrival, I went to the Salon des Indépendants.

The friend who went with me had warned me that it would be impossible to see the whole exhibition in a single day. As far as he was concerned, he came out exhausted every time he visited it. Pitying him from the bottom of my heart and following my own method, I raced through all the first rooms as if a flood were following me and made straight for the central rooms.

In this way, I saved my energy.

I made my way to the very heart of the French painting of 1910.

I attached myself to it.

No academy could have given me all I discovered by getting my teeth into the exhibitions, the shop windows, and the museums of Paris.

Beginning with the market – where, for lack of money, I bought only a piece of a long cucumber – the workman in his blue overalls, the most ardent followers of Cubism, everything showed a definite feeling for proportion, clarity, an accurate sense of form, of a more painterly kind of painting, even in the canvases of second-rate artists.

I don't know whether anyone has been able to form a clearer idea than I of the almost insurmountable difference between French painting and that of other countries before 1914. It seems to me that people abroad had very little idea of it.

As for me, I have never stopped thinking of it.

It is not a question of the degree of natural talent in an individual or a people.

Different forces were involved, largely organic or psycho-physical forces that create a predisposition towards either music, painting, literature, or sleep.

After living for some time in a studio in the Impasse du Maine, I moved into another studio more in keeping with my means, in "La Ruche" ("The Hive").

That was the name given to a hundred-odd ateliers surrounded by a small garden, close to the Vaugirard slaughterhouses. These ateliers were occupied by artistic Bohemians from all over the world.

While an offended model sobbed in the Russian ateliers; the Italian studios rang with songs and the sound of guitars, the Jewish ones with discussions, I was alone in my studio in front of my oil lamp. A studio crammed with pictures, with canvases that were not really canvases, but my tablecloths, sheets, and night-shirts torn into pieces.

Two or three o'clock in the morning. The sky is blue. Dawn is breaking. Down there, a little way off, they slaughtered cattle, cows bellowed, and I painted them.

I used to sit up like that all night long. It's already a week since the studio was cleaned out. Frames, eggshells, empty two-sou soup tins lie about higgledy-piggledy.

My lamp burned, and I with it.

It would burn until its brightness turned to a glare in the blue of morning.

It was then I climbed up to my garret. I ought to have gone down into the street and bought hot rolls on credit, but I went to bed. Later the cleaner came; I wasn't quite sure whether she came to tidy the studio (is it absolutely necessary? At least, don't touch my table!) or whether she wanted to come up and join me.

On the shelves, reproductions of El Greco and Cézanne lay next to the remains of a herring I had cut in two, the head for the first day, the tail for the next, and, thank God, a few crusts of bread.

But maybe Cendrars will come and take me out to lunch.

Before anyone entered my studio, they always had to wait. That was to give me time to put things straight, to get dressed, for I worked in the nude. In general, I can't stand clothes, I don't like putting them on, and I dress without taste.

No-one buys my pictures. I never even thought that possible.

Once only, M. Malpel offered me twenty-five francs for a picture that was on exhibition in the Salon, in the event of it not being sold.

"But exactly, why wait."

I don't know what's happened now: twenty years later the pictures are selling. They even say that a real Frenchman, Gustave Coquiot, collects my pictures.

I should see him, thank him.

And on the eve of war, I carelessly scattered nearly four hundred of my canvases in Germany, Holland, and Paris, all over the place.

Too bad. At least, since they cost them nothing, those people will go to the trouble of hanging them on their walls.


Once in Paris, I went to the Diaghilev ballet to see Bakst and Nijinsky. All his life, Diaghilev has never known whether he ought to approach me, or how.

For me, the ballets had the same source as the "Mir Iskoustwa", which, in any case, was also founded by Diaghilev. All the discoveries, the finds, the "novelties" were refined there, and polished, to reach society in a slick, sophisticated style.

As for me, I'm a son of workers, and in a drawing room, for want of something to do, I often feel like dirtying the shining floors.

The moment I opened the door to the wings, I saw Bakst in the distance.

Something brown and pink smiled at me benevolently.

Nijinsky runs up and shakes me by the shoulders. But he's already dashing off to the stage, where Karsavina is waiting for him: they were dancing the "Spectre of the Rose".

Paternally, Bakst, stops him.

"Wazia, wait, come here." And he fixes his wide scarf for him.

Near him, D'Annunzio, short, with a thin moustache, is flirting tenderly with Ida Rubinstein.

"So you came, after all?" says Bakst abruptly.

I am embarrassed. For he had advised me not to go to Paris, warning me that I was likely to die of hunger and that I must not count on him.

Yet while he was still in Petersburg, he had given me a hundred francs in the hope that I would become his assistant scene-painter. But when he saw how clumsy I was at scene-painting, he dropped me.

Nevertheless, I did leave, and here I am in front of him. I find it difficult to talk to him. I know that Bakst is extremely nervous. So am I. I am not offended. Well? should I have stayed in Russia?

There, although I was still a child, I felt at every step that I was a Jew – people made me feel it!

Whenever I had any dealings with the young artists' group, they hung my pictures (if they consented to hang them at all) in the remotest, darkest corner.

When, on Bakst's advice, I sent a few canvases to the "Mir Iskoustwa" exhibition, they were calmly left behind in the apartment of one of the members, while almost every Russian painter of any standing whatever was invited to become a member of the society.

And I thought: it must be because I'm a Jew and have no country of my own.

Paris! No word sounded sweeter to me!

To tell the truth, I didn't care whether Bakst came to see me or not, at that moment.

But as he took his leave, it was he who said:

"I'll call in on you to see what you're doing."

One day he came.

"Now," he said, "your colours sing."

These were the last words addressed by Professor Bakst to his ex-pupil.

What he saw may have convinced him that I had abandoned my ghetto and that here, in "La Ruche," in Paris, France, Europe, I am a man.

More than once, in my search for art, I wandered down the rue Laffitte, gazing at the hundreds of Renoirs, and Monets in Durand-Ruel's.

Vollard's shop particularly appealed to me. But I didn't dare go in.

In the dark, dusty windows, nothing but old newspapers and a small statue by Maillol that looked lost there. I looked for the Cézannes.

They are on the wall at the back, unframed. I press against the window, flattening my nose on it, and all of a sudden I bump into Vollard himself.

He is alone in the middle of his shop, wearing an overcoat.

I am afraid to go in. He looks bad-tempered. I daren't.

But at Bernheim's, in the place de la Madeleine, the windows are lit up as if for a wedding.

They have Van Gogh, Gauguin, Matisse.

Look around, come in and out as you please.

That's what I did, once or twice a week.

It was in the Louvre that I felt happiest.

Friends long vanished. Their prayers, my own. Their canvases light up my childish face.

Rembrandt enthralled me, Chardin, Fouquet and Géricault often brought me to a halt.

A friend from "La Ruche" produced pictures and took them to the market to sell.

One day I said to him:

"Maybe I could sell something in the market too."

He painted women in crinolines walking in a park. That didn't suit me, but why not a landscape in the style of Corot?

I took a photograph, but the more I tried to do a Corot, the farther I got from it, and I ended up in the style of Chagall!

My friend made fun of me. Imagine my surprise when I found that canvas later in an art collector's drawing room.

With a letter from Canudo, in which he praised me too highly, I went to show M. Doucet a portfolio of some fifty watercolours. I vaguely hoped he might possibly buy something.

After I had waited in his anteroom for about a quarter of an hour, his servant came in to give me back my portfolio.

"We don't need 'the best colourist of our time'," he said on his master's behalf.

Another of Canudo's letters of recommendation, to a film director, was more successful.

They were making a film which was to show a number of painters. I was one of them. We all worked in a teacher's studio. I've forgotten whether it's the teacher or one of his pupils who falls in love with the model, or the customer.

From the studio, the scene moved to a terrace on the shore of a lake, where they had set up a large table, laden with food. We took our places round the table and ate with great relish. They filmed us. I ate as much as I could.

It was worse afterwards when they proposed we should go for a boat trip, each gentleman with his lady.

My lady was a rather boring girl, not very photogenic. As the man, I had to row, which I couldn't do at all.

Our boat is far from the shore. The cameraman shoots, and shouts at me: "Go on, steer!" But there was nothing to steer. Too bad, I'm the wrong man for the job.

The girl was furious.

Nevertheless, I picked up a few francs for the day's work at the pay-desk, my costume under my arm.

I'm sorry I never saw that film.

Later, someone told me he had seen me on the screen.


In those days, one-man exhibitions were rare; Matisse and Bonnard were practically the only people to have them. The idea never even entered our heads.

I frequented the studios and academies of Montparnasse and at the same time, I was eagerly preparing for the Salons.

But how could I get such conspicuous canvases carried through "La Ruche" and right across Paris?

A good-hearted refugee took charge of everything, as much for the laughs as anything else.

On the way my handcart met the carts of others who were also taking their pictures to the Salon. They were all making for the wooden booths near the Place de l'Alma.

There, I was soon to see clearly what distinguished me from traditional French painting.

At last, the pictures are hung. In an hour, the varnishing. But the censor walks up to my pictures and orders one of them to be removed: "The Ass and the Woman".

My friend and I try to persuade him:

"But sir, it's not what you think, there's no pornography."

It's settled. The picture is hung again.

When I complained of being persecuted, even in the Salon, the wife of a doctor whom I sometimes visited for company and consolation said to me:

"Really? Well, all the better, it's what you deserve; don't paint pictures like that, then!"

I was only twenty, but I was already beginning to be afraid of people.

But the poet Rubiner came, Cendrars came, and the light in his eyes was enough to console me.

He often gave me advice, for he worried about me, but I never followed it, although he was right.

He persuaded me that I could work peacefully side by side with arrogant cubists, to whom I must have been a nobody.

They didn't bother me. I looked at them out of the corner of my eye and thought:

"Let them choke themselves with their square pears on their triangular tables!"

No doubt my early tendencies were a little strange to the French. And I regarded them so lovingly! It was painful.

But perhaps my art, I thought, is a wild art, a blazing mercury, a blue soul leaping up on my canvases.

And I thought: "Down with naturalism, impressionism, and realistic cubism!"

They cramp me and make me sad.

All the questions are brought up again – volume, perspective, Cézanne, Negro sculpture.

Where are we going? What is this age that sings hymns to technical art and makes a god of formalism?

May our folly be welcomed!

An expiatory bath. A revolution in depths, not only on the surface.

Don't call me fanciful! On the contrary, I am a realist. I love the earth.


I broke from the fences of my native town for a while, and here I am, at large in the circles and salons of French poets and painters.

There is Canudo. Black beard, blazing eyes.

Every Friday at his home you will meet Gleizes, Metzinger, La Fresnaye, Léger, Raynal, Valentine de Saint-Point, accompanied by her three young admirers; Segonzac, a teacher at the "La Palette" academy, where I sometimes worked; Lhote, Luc-Albert Moreau, and so many others. It was nice and warm there.

Delaunay was particularly active. I couldn't really understand him. At the Salon, it was the size of his canvases that struck me. He carried them triumphantly to the end of the stands, and winked, which meant: "Well?"

Canudo gave me a warm welcome, and I shall never forget him.

He took me here and there, and even organized an exhibition of my drawings in his sitting room one evening, spreading them out on tables and armchairs, all over the place.

Once, in the café, he said to me:

"Your head reminds me of Christ's." And grabbing a newspaper, he flung it on the floor:

"Blast! There's nothing about me in it!"

With you I plunge into the depths of Montjoie. As if dazzling lights shone out around you. As if a flight of white sea-gulls, or flakes of snowy white were mounting up to the sky in strands.

There, another light, resonant flame – Blaise, my friend Cendrars.

A chrome smock, socks of different colours. Floods of sunshine, poverty, and rhymes.

Webs of colour. Of blazing, liquid art. The ferment of newly begun pictures. Heads, disjointed limbs, flying cows.

I remember all that – and you, Cendrars?

He was the first to come and see me at "La Ruche".

He read me his poems, looking out of the open window, smiled at my pictures to my face, and we both laughed.

There was André Salmon. But where is he?

I can hear his name. His pale face glows. I have just shaken hands with him.

There's Max Jacob. He looks like a Jew.

He looked like that beside Apollinaire.

One day we went to lunch together not far from "La Ruche".

I wasn't sure whether he had so much as forty sous in his pocket. And did he think I had enough to pay for the meal?

We had salad, sauce, salt, everything that began with "s".

Afterwards, we climbed slowly up to his place in Montmartre. He had plenty of free time, and I had even more.

At last, his apartment, his courtyard, his dark corner, the entrance at the side – a real little Witebsk yard. Small pictures hang in the entrance, right up to the door.

What did we talk about? In what language?

I understood very little. To tell the truth, I was scared.

His eyes flashed and rolled all the time. His body twitched and tossed. Suddenly he calmed down. His mouth moved, half-opened, whistled. He smiled, and his eyes, his chin, his arms, spoke to me, won me over.

I said to myself: "If I follow him, he'll swallow me whole and throw my bones out of the window."


This is the garret of Apollinaire, that gentle Zeus.

He blazed a trail for us in verse, numbers, and flowing syllables.

He came out of his corner room with a smile that gradually spread all over his face. His nose was sharply pointed and his gentle, mysterious eyes sang of pleasure.

He carried his stomach like a volume of collected works and his legs gesticulated like arms.

In his room, there were a great many discussions.

A little man is sitting in one corner,

Apollinaire goes over to him and wakes him up:

"Do you know what we ought to do, Monsieur Walden? We ought to organize an exhibition of this young man's works. Don't you know him . . . ? Monsieur Chagall . . . ?

One day, Apollinaire and I go out together to lunch at Baty's, in Montparnasse.

On the way, he suddenly stopped:

"Look, there's Degas. He's crossing the road. He's blind."

Degas was striding along alone, frowning, looking surly, leaning heavily on his cane.

During lunch, I asked Apollinaire why he didn't introduce me to Picasso.

"Picasso? Do you want to commit suicide? All his friends end up like that," replied Apollinaire, smiling as he always did.

"What a colossal appetite," I thought, as I watched him eat.

Perhaps he has to eat so much to feed his mind. Maybe talent consists in eating. Simply eat and drink, and perhaps the rest will come of its own accord. As he ate, Apollinaire seemed to sing, and the food rang in his mouth.

The wine tinkled in his glass, the meat clattered between his teeth. At the same time, he was waving to right and left. Acquaintances on all sides.

Oh! Oh! Oh! Ah! Ah! Ah!

And at the slightest pause, he emptied his glass, resplendent in his table napkin.

When lunch was over, we staggered back to "La Ruche", licking our lips.

"Have you never been here before?"

"This is where the Bohemians, Italians and Jews live; there are some girls, too. Maybe we'll find Cendrars at the café on the corner, in the Passage de Dantzig.

"We'll surprise him. He'll open his mouth as wide as two eggs, and hastily hide sheets of newly written verse in his pockets.

"It's not far from the slaughterhouse, where skilful toughs savagely slaughter my poor cows."

I daren't show my canvases to Apollinaire.

"I know, you are the one who inspired cubism. But I want something else."

What else? I am embarrassed.

We walk down the dark corridor where water drips continually, where piles of rubbish are heaped up.

A round landing; about a dozen numbered doors.

I open mine.

Apollinaire enters cautiously, as if he were afraid the whole building might suddenly collapse and bury him in its ruins.

Personally, I do not think a scientific bent is good for art.

Impressionism and cubism are alien to me.

Art seems to me to be a state of soul, more than anything else.

The soul of all is sacred, the soul of every biped in every place on earth.

Only the upright heart that has its own logic and reason is free.

The soul that has reached the level that men call literature, the illogical, of its own accord, is the purest.

I am not speaking of the old realism, or of romanticism – symbolism, which has contributed very little; nor of mythology or fantasy of any kind, but of what, my God?

You will say, those schools are no more than formal trappings.

Primitive art already possessed the technical perfection that present generations strive for, juggling and even sinking into stylization.

I liken those formal trappings to the Pope of Rome, magnificently clothed, beside the naked Christ, or to an ornate church beside prayers in the open fields.

Apollinaire sits down. He reddens, puffs out, smiles, and murmurs: "Supernatural . . . !

The next day I received a letter, a poem dedicated to me: "Rodztag".

The meaning of your words strikes us like beating rain.

Surely you are dreaming today of watercolours, of the new surface of painting, of poets with outrageous destinies, of all of us, whom you once named.

Has he gone, has he perished, or is he still here, with that dazzling smile on his mortal face?

And my days drag by on the Place de la Concorde, or near the Jardin du Luxembourg.

I look at Danton and Watteau, I tear off leaves.

Oh! If only I could trace my way in the sky with my arms and legs, riding on the stone chimera of Notre Dame!

There it is! Paris, you are my second Witebsk!


I often said: I am no artist. What then – a cow?

What of it? I even thought of putting my picture on my visiting cards.

It seemed that the cow was conducting world politics at that time.

Cubism chopped her up, expressionism twisted her.

And suddenly, in the East, those forebodings were fulfilled.

I saw with my own eyes how the paintings of Derain, Juan Gris, and others cracked in the Kahnweiler Gallery. The paint peeled off.

It seemed that I carried the first signs of that stormy period with me to Berlin, where I went to see my exhibition.

My canvases, unframed, were hung close together in

two small rooms in the editorial offices of the review *Sturm;* about a hundred of my watercolours were simply spread out on tables.

My pictures swelled in the Potsdammerstrasse, while cannon were being loaded nearby.

Can we help it if we can only see world events through canvas, paint, and painting materials, thickening and vibrating like poisonous gases?

Europe goes to war. Picasso, no more cubism.

Who cares about Serbia? Attack all those barefoot peasants!

Set Russia afire and all of us with her ...


As I was in Berlin, I didn't realize that, within a month, the bloody comedy would begin that was to transform the whole world, and Chagall with it, into a new stage on which immense crowd scenes would be played.

No presentiment disturbed me enough to stop me making a trip to Russia.

I had been wanting to go for three months; I wanted to go to my sister's wedding, for one thing, and, for another, to see "her" again.

This fourth and last romance had almost evaporated during the four years I had spent abroad. At the end of my stay in Paris, all that remained of it was a bundle of letters. Another year, and everything might have been over between us.

After a brief stay in Berlin, I left for Russia.

No sooner had I arrived in Vilna than I said to a Frenchwoman who was my travelling companion:

"Look, this is Russia." Particularly as the porter was about to disappear with all my luggage.

The Tzar was honouring Odessa with a visit and was receiving delegations at the station. It was impossible to get out.

I remembered how we schoolchildren were taken near town to greet the Tzar, who had come to Witebsk to review the regiments that were about to leave for the front (the Russo-Japanese war).

We set out well before dawn.

Crowds of sleepy, excited boys passed one another on the road, making their way in long columns towards the snow-covered fields.

We lined up along the high road.

And we stood like that for hours with our feet in the snow, waiting for the Imperial procession to arrive.

For fear of an attempt on the Tzar's life, the train had been stopped in the open fields.

At last, the Tzar appeared in the distance, very pale, in a private's uniform.

Every one of us would have liked to get a closer look at him, but as we were herded together like sheep, we couldn't possibly move.

Suddenly, a little fellow slipped out of the rows of schoolchildren. He went towards the Tzar, holding a petition above his head.

In an instant, Nicholas was enveloped in a cloud of princes, ministers, and generals, glittering in their ceremonial dress. Tall, robust, white-haired or bald, chests bulging with medals, severe or smiling, they followed the Tzar on horseback or on foot.

It was snowing lightly. The cheers of thousands of soldiers re-echoed in the distance, and close at hand. The frozen air absorbed the national anthem, sometimes transforming it into doleful sounds. The bands played continually, in several places at once.

Covered with snow, the Tzar marched at the head of the army, giving a slight salute.

One after another, the regiments filed past him and left for the front.


"But what a shambles this town is! And here we are, stuck on the station!" I said to my companion.

"Poor things, especially you . . ."

"Don't worry, I'll put you on the train. And you'll get to your senator's house in Tzarskoye where you're going to be governess."

Was this Russia, already?

I didn't really know Russia well.

Had I ever seen it? Where are Novgorod, Rostov, Kiev? Where, where are they?

All I've seen is Petrograd, Moscow, the little village of Lyozno, and Witebsk.

Witebsk is a place apart; a town unlike any other, an unhappy town, a boring town.

A town full of girls, who, for lack of time or courage, I never even approached.

Dozens, hundreds of synagogues, butcher's shops, passers-by.

Was that Russia?

It's only my town, mine, which I have rediscovered.

I come back to it with emotion.

It was at that time that I painted my Witebsk series of 1914. I painted everything that met my eyes. I painted at my window, I never walked down the street without my box of paints.

A hedge, a stake, a floor or a chair was enough for me.

Look: at the table, in front of the samovar, a meek old man is leaning back in his chair.

I look at him questioningly: "Who are you?"

"Why, don't you know me? Have you never heard of the preacher from Slousk?"

"Then listen; in that case, please come round to my house. I'll make you . . . How can I put it . . ."

How could I explain to him? I was afraid he might get up and go.

He came, sat down on a chair, and promptly fell asleep.

Have you seen the old man in green I painted? That's him.

Another old man passes our house. Grey hair, a surly look. A sack on his back.

I wonder: is he even capable opening his mouth to beg?

Indeed, he doesn't talk. He comes in and stands discreetly by the door. He stands there for a long time. And if no-one gives him anything, he leaves without a word, as he came.

"Listen," I tell him, "have a little rest. Sit down. Like that. You don't mind that, do you? Have a rest. I'll give you twenty kopecks. Just put on my father's prayer clothes and sit down."

Have you seen my portrait of the old man praying?
That's him.

It was good, when you could work in peace. Sometimes
I was confronted with a face so old and tragic that it looked
almost angelic.

But I couldn't keep it up for more than half-an-hour.
He stank too much.

"That's all, sir, you may go."

Have you seen my old man reading? That's him.

I painted and painted, and finally, one rainy night, in
spite of my protests, I found myself standing under the
most authentic of wedding crowns, like those in my
pictures.

But a long comedy had preceded the ceremony. Here it
is.

The parents and the many relatives of my, yes . . . yes
. . . of my wife, did not approve of my background.

Why not? My father, a simple storeman. My grandfather. . .

As for them – just think, they owned three jewellery
shops in our town. The many-coloured fires of rings,
brooches, and bracelets glittered and sparkled in their

windows. Clocks and alarms were ringing all over the place.

Being used to different surroundings, I thought it fantastic.

At their house, three times a week, they made enormous applecakes, cheesecakes and poppy-cakes, at the sight of which I would have fainted. And at breakfast they served mounds of those cakes, which everyone attacked furiously, in an ecstasy of greed. And in our house, a simple still life, like those of Chardin.

Their father ate grapes the way mine ate onions; and poultry, which was sacrificed no more than once a year in our house, on the eve of the Day of Atonement, was always on their table.

Her grandfather, a white-haired old man with a long beard, prowls about the apartment, looking for Russian books, Russian passports, and throws everything he finds into the stove, burns it.

He can't stand his grandchildren going to Russian schools.

Useless, useless!

To the cheder with all of them, to become rabbis!

He does nothing but pray all day.

And on the Day of Atonement, he is out of his mind.

But he's already too old to fast.

The chief rabbi himself has authorized him to take a few drops of milk on the fast day.

My wife holds the spoon for him.

He is bathed in tears, his tears trickle down his beard into his milk.

He is in despair. The spoon, shaking, scarcely wets his lips on the fast day.

I can say no more. My head is spinning.

My fiancée's mother told her daughter:

"Listen, I think he even puts rouge on his cheeks. What kind of husband will that boy make you? He's as pink as a girl. He'll never be able to earn his living."

But what can be done if that's the way she likes him. Impossible to convince her.

"You'll ruin yourself with him, my daughter. You'll ruin yourself for nothing.

"Besides, he's an artist. Whatever's that?"

"And what will people say?"

This was the way my fiancée's family argued about me, and, morning and night, she brought sweet cakes to my studio from her house, broiled fish, boiled milk, all sorts of decorative materials, and even some boards which I used for an easel.

I only had to open my window, and blue air, love, and flowers entered with her.

Dressed all in white or all in black, she has long been flying over my canvases, guiding my art.

I never complete a picture or an engraving without asking for her "yes" or "no".

So what do I care about her parents, her brothers. God protect them!

My poor father.

"Papa," I say "come to my wedding!"

He, like me, would rather have gone to bed.

Was it worth while getting involved with such high-class people?

On arriving, very late, at my fiancée's house, I found a whole sanhedrin already assembled there.

A pity I'm not Veronese.

Around the long table, the chief rabbi – a rather cunning old man – a few fat, important-looking bourgeois, a whole galaxy of humble Jews, whose stomachs were aching in anticipation of my arrival and . . . dinner. For without me, there would be no dinner. I knew it, and was amused by their agitation.

What does it matter to those gluttons that this is the most important night of my life, that soon, without music, against the yellow background of the wall, without stars and without sky, under a red canopy, I shall be married!

And as that solemn hour drew near, I turned pale in the midst of the crowd.

Relatives, friends, acquaintances and servants were sitting down and standing up, coming and going.

Tears, smiles, confetti, were already ripening in their breasts. All the right things to shed on the fiancé.

They were waiting for me, and as they waited, they chattered.

They were embarrassed to learn that "he" was an artist.

"It seems he's already famous, too . . . And he even gets paid for his pictures. Did you know?"

"All the same, that's no living," sighs another.

"What do you mean? What about the honour and glory?"

"Who's his father then?" enquires a third.

"Ah! I know." They fell silent.

I felt that if they had put me in a coffin, my features would have been softer, less stiff than the mask that sat down beside my future wife.

How I regretted the foolish shyness that prevented me from touch that mountain of grapes, of fruit, the countless delicious dishes that decorated the great wedding table.

Half-an-hour later (what am I saying, well before, the sanhedrin was in a hurry), blessings, wine, or perhaps curses rained down on our heads, framed in the red canopy.

It was driving me mad. Everyone was spinning round me.

With emotion, I clasped my wife's slender, bony hands. I wanted to run away to the country with her, to kiss her and burst out laughing.

But after the nuptial blessing, my brothers-in-law took me back to my house, while their sister, my wife, remained at her parent's home.

This was the height of ritual perfection.

Alone together in the country at last.

Woods, pine trees, solitude. The moon behind the forest. The pig in the sty, the horse outside the window, in the fields. The sky lilac.

It was not only a honeymoon, but also a milk-moon.

A herd of cows belonging to the army was pastured not far from us. Every morning, the soldiers sold bucketfuls of milk for a few kopecks. My wife, who had been brought up chiefly on cakes, made me drink it all. So that by autumn, I could hardly button my coats.

Around midday, our room looked like a superb panel in one of the great salons of Paris.

I was the winner. I chased a mouse that leapt triumphantly on to my easel. Then my wife thought:

"So he is capable of killing something."

But the war was rumbling over me. And Europe closed before my very eyes.

I finger the Paris certificate in my pocket and hurry to the governor of the town to ask for permission to leave.

I come out again sadly with my papers stamped and sealed.

I felt as if I were covered with whiskers or fur, as if I were completely naked.

My Paris!

What does the governor know about painting?

Trains swarming with soldiers. Broad faces with high cheek-bones, grey and dusty.

They clung to the steps, climbed on to them and on to the roofs of the carriages.

They were going to Sebez, to Mohileff, they were moving up to the front.

Why don't they call me up?

I must wait my turn.

And what shall I do out there? Stare at the fields, the trees, the sky, the clouds, blood and guts?

It looked as if they didn't even want me. I'm not reliable. I'm good for nothing. I haven't even any flesh on me. And colours – pink in the cheeks, blue in the eyes – colours don't make a soldier.

Soldiers, moujiks in woollen caps, with laptis on their feet, pass in front of me. They eat, they stink. The smell of the front, the stench of herrings, tobacco, fleas.

I hear, I feel the battles, the gunfire, the soldiers buried in the trenches.

The first prisoners arrive.

There's a fat, athletic-looking German with several months' growth of beard; he is sullen and sleepy.

If it were not wartime, I'd have approached him and asked him for news of Walden, of my pictures imprisoned in Germany.

Another wounded man looks at me with an air of reproach. He is pale, he is old and thin, like my bearded grandfather.

# 13

What was I to do? In the meantime, I had to settle down somewhere. In Petrograd, perhaps?

To tell the truth, I didn't fancy going there. In the country where we spent the summer, the chief rabbi, Schneersohn, lived too.

People from all the surrounding villages came to consult him. Each with his own troubles.

Some wanted to avoid military service, and came to ask his advice. Others, distressed at having no children, came to ask his blessing. Some, puzzled by a passage in the Talmud, wanted explanations. Or else they came simply to see him, to try and get close to him. How do I know?

But certainly no artist had ever signed his visitors' list.

My God! Bewildered, but worried about where I should live, I also ventured to go and ask the learned rabbi's advice (I remembered the rabbi's songs my mother used to sing on Sabbath evenings).

Was he really a saint?

In summer, he lived in this part of the country, and his

house reminded one of an old synagogue surrounded by mezzanines, annexes for his followers and for his staff.

On reception days, his anteroom was full of people.

One got crushed in the midst of the noise and the gossip.

But a good tip got you in more easily.

The porter informs me that the rabbi does not often converse with mere mortals. I must put all my questions in writing and hand him the note as soon as I crossed his threshold.

No explanations.

At last my turn came, and the door in front of me was opened. Pushed by that antheap of people, I found myself in a vast green room.

Square, almost empty, silent.

At the end, a long table littered with notes, sheets of paper, requests, prayers, money. Only the rabbi is seated.

A candle flares. He glances at the note. His face.

"So you would like to go to Petrograd, my son? You think you will like it there. So be it my son, I bless you. Go there."

"But Rabbi," I say, "I would rather stay in Witebsk. My parents and my wife's parents live there, you know, there."

"Ah! Well, my son, since you prefer Witebsk, I bless you, go there."

I would have liked to continue the conversation.

So many questions were on the tip of my tongue.

I wanted to talk to him about art in general, and mine in particular. Perhaps he would instil a little of the divine spirit into me. Who knows?

And to ask him if the Israelites are really God's chosen people, as it says in the Bible. And also to know what he thought about Christ, whose pale face had long been troubling me.

Without looking round, I reached the door and went out.

I ran to my wife. It was moonlight. The dogs barked. And there was nothing better than. . .

My God! What sort of a rabbi are you, Rabbi Schneersohn!

Since then, whatever advice I am given, I do exactly the opposite.

I could simply have stayed in that village, and blindly followed that same rabbi, who was returning to his headquarters in the little suburb of Lubawitchy.

But with the war and the enlistment of my age group. . .

What was I to do? My wife preferred large towns. She loves culture. She is right.

Doesn't she have enough trouble with me?

I shall never understand why men crowd together in the same places when, outside the towns, there are tens of thousands of empty miles stretching out on all sides.

I should be satisfied with a hole of some kind, a secluded spot. I'd be so happy there.

I would sit down in a synagogue and look. Just that. Or on a bench beside a river, or else I should visit.

And I should paint, paint pictures that might surprise the whole world.

No.

One fine evening (it's always a fine evening), one rainy evening, it's my turn to climb into a carriage swarming with soldiers, all cursing and fighting for a seat.

I can hardly keep my place on the steps. The train moves off. I push against a back, hanging on to another soldier's shoulders. The train pulls out.

The lucky devils inside puff out their chests and give advice:

"Give him" (they mean me) "a punch, and that's it."

A single push of their backs weighted with kit-bags would have been enough to send me flying like an arrow over the rails into the dark, snowy fields.

I hold the rail tighter, my hands freeze. I fly, and the train flies with me.

My overcoat billows out in the wind like a parachute and crackles with cold.

In this way I arrive in Petrograd. What use is that?

There I found the haven of grace that the war had reserved for me – a military office. There, I scribbled on paper.

My boss made war on me.

Being my brother-in-law, he was always afraid people would blame him for my inefficiency, so he kept a particularly close watch on me.

He would come up to me and ask for some piece of information. Alas! As I could hardly ever supply it, he would sweep all my papers aside and shout, in a frenzy:

"What system have you, then? What have you done? Are you telling me, Marc Zacharowitch, that you don't even know that? And it's a mere trifle!" Seeing him in such a rage, eyes and cheeks blazing, I felt sorry for him.

I smiled to myself.

Yet in the end he managed to implant a new talent in me: after that, I knew, after a fashion, how to find my way around my registers, both for entrants and leavers. I even cooked reports.


By comparison with my military office, the front looked like a cakewalk to me, like exercises in the open air.

Towards evening, I went home, unhappy.

I could almost have cried.

I told my wife of my sufferings. She suffered in silence.

I was glad when, on certain evenings, I could at least do a little painting and talk about it with my friend, the doctor-writer Baal-Machschowess-Eljacheff.

His friendship was a joy to me, particularly at that time.

We met at the home of Kagan-Chabchaj, the collector, where there were heated discussions about art.

He was one of the first collectors to buy some of my pictures, for the purpose of founding a national museum.

Every evening, we went out with Eljacheff; as we wandered through the little alleys of Moscow at night, he spread the sparks of his eloquence before me.

When he swung round towards me in the darkness, his glasses gleamed.

His little black moustache, his keen, penetrating eyes held my gaze.

Both sceptical and kindly, he listened, talked, argued, waving his arms, limping slightly.

We became firm friends.

And if I happened to stay the night with him, he never stopped talking until morning, by the dim glow of the night-light that stood by my bed. He talked of writers, the war, life in general, art, the Revolution, his nephew, a People's Commissar, and particularly of his wife, who had left him.

He had met her when she was very young. She was exceptionally beautiful. Black eyes, smooth skin, tall and slim, she was as silent as a statue.

Neither my friend's writing, nor his love, made any impression on her. Indifferent, she accepted his favours coldly. And one fine day, she left him, and ran away with someone else.

"Of course," said my friend, "she needs a man who can satisfy her completely, you see. And just look at me: paralysed in one side, and when I talk, I slobber."

In the mornings, he waited for patients. In vain.

Then he began writing.

He shared his ration of horsemeat with us more than once during those years of famine and cold. We feasted on it in his kitchen. His son played beside us. His father brought him up as best he could.

With a glass of tea in his trembling hands, he would talk, talk, talk. His tea spills; it went cold long ago. I drink mine and he, still talking, adjusts his glasses, which almost fell into the tea, chilled between his icy hands.

I also showed my pictures to another friend, the venerable Syrkine.

He was so short-sighted that he had to arm himself with a pair of binoculars before he could see anything, and when he met you, he bumped into you.

He defended me with devotion.

Where are you today?

# 14

The Germans were carrying off their first victories. The poisonous gases choked me even at Lyteiny Prospect 46, the headquarters of my military office.

My painting lost its edge.

One very dark night, I went out alone. Not a soul in the street. The cobblestones on the road stood out distinctly.

It seems there is a pogrom in the centre.

A gang of ruffians is on the loose.

In military greatcoats, with shoulders and buttons ripped off, that dubious gang roamed the streets, amusing themselves by throwing passers-by into the water from the top of the bridge. You could hear the shooting.

I was curious to see this pogrom at close quarters.

I creep forward. The street lamps are out. I feel panicky, especially in front of butcher's windows. There you can see calves that are still alive lying beside the butcher's hatchets and knives. Locked up for their last night, they bleat piteously.

All of a sudden, a gang of five or six looters comes round the corner, armed to the teeth.

The moment they see me, they ask:

"Jew or not?"

For a second, I hesitate. It is dark.

My pockets are empty, my fingers sensitive, my legs weak, and they are out for blood. My death would be futile. I so much wanted to live.

"All right! Get along!" they shout.

Without further delay I hurried towards the centre where the pogrom had broken out.

Gunshots. Bodies fall into the water.

I run home.

I prayed: "Wilhelm, be satisfied with Warsaw, with Kowno, don't enter Dwinsk! And whatever you do, don't touch Witebsk! That's where I am, painting my pictures."

But luckily for Wilhelm, the Russians fought badly. Although they fought furiously, they could not drive the enemy back. Our men excel only in the attack.

Every defeat of the army was an excuse for its leader, Grand Duke Nicholas Nicolaewitch, to blame the Jews.

"Get them all out within twenty-four hours. Or have them shot. Or both at once!"

The army advanced, and as they advanced, the Jewish population retreated, abandoning towns and villages. I felt like having them all put on to my canvases, to keep them safe.

Fists were being shaken at the sky.

Soldiers fled the front. The war, ammunitions, fleas, everything was left behind in the trenches.

Panic-stricken soldiers broke carriage windows, commandeered wrecked trains and, packed like herrings, bolted towards the towns, towards the capitals.

Freedom roared on their lips. Oaths hissed.

I don't stay put either. I desert the office, the inkwells, and all the records. Goodbye!

I also leave the front, with the others.

Freedom and the end of the war.

Freedom. Absolute freedom.

And the February Revolution breaks out.

My first feeling – is that I won't have to have any more dealings with the "passportist".

The Volunsky regiment was the first to mutiny.

I ran to Znamensky Square, from there to Liteynay, to Nevsky, and back.

Gunfire everywhere. The cannon were being mounted. They were laying out the arms.

"Three cheers for the Duma! Three cheers for the provisional government!"

The gunners voted for the people.

After limbering up their cannons, they left. The other corps swear allegiance, one after the other. After them, the officers, the sailors.

In front of the Duma, President Rodzianko thunders:

"Don't forget, brothers, the enemy is still at our gates. Swear allegiance! Swear!"

"We swear! Hurrah!"

They shouted themselves hoarse.

Something was about to be born.

I was living in a kind of coma.

I never even heard Kerensky. He was at the height of his fame. Hand on chest, like Napoleon, his glance too. He sleeps in the Imperial bed.

The Constitutional Democratic ministry is succeeded by the ministry of the semi-Democrats. Then the Democrats. They joined forces. Checkmate.

After that, General Korniloff tried to save Russia. The deserters attacked the whole railway system.

"Back to our homes!"

That was in the month of June. The R.S. party was in favour. Tchernoff was making speeches in the amphitheatre.

"Constituent assembly, constituent assembly!"

In Znamensky Square in front of the great monument of Alexander III, people were beginning to whisper:

"Lenin's arrived."

"Who's he?"

"Lenin from Geneva?"

"Himself."

"He's here."

"Not really?"

"Down with him! Drive him out! Three cheers for the provisional government! All power to the constituent assembly!"

"Is it true he came from Germany in an armoured carriage?"

The actors and painters have gathered in the Michailowsky Theatre. They mean to found a Ministry of Arts.

I attend as an onlooker.

Suddenly I hear my own name proposed for minister by the young artists.

I leave Petrograd and return to my Witebsk. I still prefer my home town to being a minister.

Seeing me neglect painting, my wife wept. She warned me that it would all end in insults, in snubs.

It was so.

Unfortunately, she is always right.

When will I learn to take her advice?

ПРОЩАЙТЕ!

## 15

Russia was covered with ice.

Lenin turned her upside down the way I turn my pictures.

Madame Kchessinsky has left. Lenin is making a speech from his balcony.

Everyone is there. The letters R.S.F.S.R. were already turning red. The factories were stopping.

The horizons opened.

Space and emptiness.

No more bread. The black lettering on the morning posters made me sick at heart.

Coup d'état. Lenin president of the Sownarkom. Lunat-charsky president of the Narkompross.

Trotsky is there too. And Zinowieff. Uritsky guards the entrances to the constituent assembly.

Everyone is there and I – I'm at Witebsk.

I can go without food for several days and sit beside a mill watching the bridge, the beggars, and the poor wretches weighed down with bundles.

I can linger in front of the public baths and watch the soldiers and their wives coming out with birch twigs in their hands.

I can wander beside the river, beside the cemetery...

I can forget you, Vladimir Ilytch, you, Lenin, and Trotsky too...

And instead of all that, instead of painting my pictures in peace, I have founded a School of Fine Arts and become its director, its president, and everything else.

"What bliss!"

"What folly!" thought my wife.


The Narkom, Lunatcharsky, receives me smilingly at his office in the Kremlin.

I met him once in Paris, shortly before the war. He was a journalist. He came to my studio, in "La Ruche".

Spectacles, a short beard, the mask of a faun.

He came to see my pictures to write an article for a newspaper.

I've heard he is a Marxist. But my knowledge of Marxism was limited to knowing that Marx was a Jew, and that he had a long white beard. Now I was aware that my art was unlikely to agree with him.

I said to Lunatcharsky:

"Whatever you do, don't ask me why I painted in blue or green, and why you can see a calf inside the cow's belly, etc. On the other hand, you're welcome: if Marx is so wise, let him come back to life and explain it himself."

I showed him my canvases, going through them at lightning speed.

He smiled and silently took notes in his notebook.

I have a feeling he has always had an unpleasant memory of this visit, and always will.

And now he solemnly confirms me in my new functions.

I return to Witebsk on the eve of the first anniversary of the October Revolution.

My town, like the others, is preparing to celebrate it by decorating the streets with great posters.

In our town there were quite a few house-painters.

I called them all together, young and old, and told them:

"Listen; you and your children are all to be pupils in my school.

"Close down your sign studios and daub-shops. All the orders will be sent on to our school, and you will divide them between you.

"Here are a dozen sketches. Copy them on big canvases and, on the day the workers' parade comes through town with flags and torches, hang them out on the walls of the town and the suburbs."

All those house-painters, the old bearded ones and their apprentices alike, began to copy my cows and my horses.

And on October 25th, my multicoloured animals swung all over the town, swollen with revolution.

The workers marched up singing the International.

When I saw them smile, I was sure they understood me.

The leaders, the Communists, seemed less gratified.

Why is the cow green and why is the horse flying through the sky, why?

What's the connection with Marx and Lenin?

People were besieging the young sculptors with orders for busts of Lenin and Marx, in cement.

I fear they may have melted in the Witebsk rain.

Poor town!

When they erected that timid cast, done by a pupil from

the school, in the public gardens, I hid behind the bushes and grinned.

Where is Marx, where is he?

Where is the bench where I used to kiss you?

Where can I sit to hide my shame?

One Marx was not enough.

They put up another one, in another street.

It was no more successful.

Big and heavy, it was even less benevolent and frightened the coachmen who stood at the rank opposite.

I was ashamed. Was it my fault?

Wearing a Russian blouse, with a leather case under my arm, I looked every inch the Soviet civil servant.

Only my long hair, and the pink marks on my cheeks that came off my pictures, betrayed the painter.

My eyes blaze with administrative fire. I am surrounded by boys – pupils I'm preparing to turn into geniuses in twenty-four hours.

I struggle to get the grants the school needs, to procure money, paints, equipment. I am continually making arrangements to get them exempted from military service.

I was always out on errands. My wife deputized for me in my absence.

I went to the Goubispolkom meetings to ask for subsidies from the town.

While I was explaining my project, the president of the Soviet deliberately fell asleep.

He only woke up at the end of my account, and then he asked:

"What do you think, Comrade Chagall, is it more important to have an emergency repair done to the bridge or to give money to your School of Fine Arts?"

Every time I received grants, thanks to Lunatcharsky's

support, he insisted that I should at least bow to his authority. Otherwise, he threatened me with prison.

But I never agreed to that.

From time to time, other commissars came to see me.

To remind myself that they were still boys who only put on an impressive manner at meetings and pounded on the table, I amused myself by whacking them on the back or on the behind — both the military commissar, an adolescent of nineteen, and the commissar of public works. Although they were strong fellows, particularly the former, they quickly admitted defeat and I sat down triumphantly on the military commissar's back.

All that reinforced the town authorities' respect for the arts. But it did not prevent them from arresting my mother-in-law along with all the other citizens, simply because they were rich.

In the course of my essential visits, I had occasion to go to Maxim Gorki's house.

I don't know what he made of me.

When I entered his house, I saw pictures on the walls that were so devoid of taste I thought I must have taken the wrong door.

He was lying in bed and spitting, sometimes into his handkerchief and sometimes into a spittoon.

He accepted all my plans without discussion, with an air of surprise; as he watched me, he tried to work out where I came from and who I was.

And I had forgotten what I had come to ask for.

A man only had to express the wish, and I immediately took pity on him and invited him to teach in my school. For I wanted all the trends in art to be represented there.

One of them, whom I had actually appointed director, spent his time sending parcels off to his family. In the post office, and even in the Communist committee, people were beginning to talk about the teachers taken on by Comrade Chagall.

Another amused herself by flirting with commissars of the town, accepting their favours willingly. When reports of this reached me, I was furious.

"How can you?" I demanded feverishly.

But she answered slyly:

"Why, Comrade Chagall, I do it for your sake! ... to help you."

A third teacher, who lived in the school itself, surrounded himself with women smitten with "suprematic" mysticism.

How he attracted them, I don't know.

Another one, my most ardent disciple, swore friendship and devotion to me. You would have thought I was his Messiah. But as soon as he was appointed a teacher, he went over to the enemy camp and heaped abuse and ridicule on me.

He was already worshipping a new god, whom he soon rejected, having betrayed him in his turn.

There was another old friend, a schoolmate.

I had sent for him to come and be my assistant. He was working in an office of some kind.

What's the use of that, I thought, he's wasting his time there.

I took him on.

He was glad, and as a token of his gratitude, he wasted no time in going over to the enemy's side.

As president I was obliged to hold meetings late at night. Ardently, I urged the teachers to do their duties; but they gradually nodded and fell asleep.

They sniggered a lot about those meetings, even about the school, about me, and my convictions.

It is true, I didn't have much patience. I called on them to speak, but as I knew in advance what they were going to say, I never let them finish. I wanted to establish school, museum, communal studios all at once.

I was impatient to see everything working. I did not spare myself, nor the others.

As all the teachers "adored" one another, they began to "adore" me too.

I became a celebrity in the town and I turned out dozens of painters.

# 16

One day when I was off on one of my usual expeditions to get bread, paints, and money for them, all the teachers rebelled and drew my pupils into their rebellion.

God forgive them!

And with the support of all those I had welcomed, assured of bread and employment, they passed a resolution deciding that I should be expelled from the school within twenty-four hours.

After I left, they immediately calmed down.

There was no-one left to fight. After appropriating all the school property, even the pictures I had bought from them and paid for on behalf of the State with the intention of founding a museum in Witebsk, they scattered, leaving the school and the pupils to the hazards of fate.

I could laugh. Why rake up all this old rubbish?

I shall say no more of friends and enemies.

Their features are embedded in my heart like blocks of wood.

Make me leave within twenty-four hours with all my family!

Have my signs and notices taken down, stutter as much as you like!

Never fear, I shall not remember you.

If I devoted myself entirely to the needs of my native land for several years, neglecting my own work, it was not for love of you, but for my town, for my father, for my mother, who lie buried there.

As for you, leave me in peace.

I shan't be surprised if, after I have been absent for a long time, my town obliterates every trace of me and forgets me and forgets the man who put his own paint-brushes aside, fretted, suffered, and took the trouble to sow the seeds of Art there, who dreamt of transforming ordinary houses into museums and the common man into a creator.

And then I understood that no man is a prophet in his own country.

I left for Moscow.


I think of my friends. Were they really friends?

My first childhood friend, whom I loved so dearly, left me, dropping away like a piece of gauze from a wound.

Why?

Even while he was a pupil in the School of Fine Arts, he appropriated the studies I did in class, rubbed out my signature and passed them off as his own. I did not reproach him. But the board turned him out, all the same.

Later, while I was living in Paris, he set himself to steal my fiancée, trying to win her over by pretending to love her.

And finally, when he saw my adult canvases, and no longer understood me, he grew jealous, like all the others.

In this way our childhood friendship evaporated on the threshold of unkind adult life.

It wasn't even a friendship, a friend.

Then with whom shall I make friends? Whom shall I love?

So my doors are open now.

My soul too, even my smile, sometimes.

I'm no longer surprised when people abandon me, when I am betrayed, and I no longer rejoice in new acquaintances. I am on my guard.

Not a single friend. Another one also left me. He is no longer poor, in fact he is famous.

But the world is full of friends.

When it snows, I open my mouth to swallow it.

Have I got it?

Friends are like that.

May God help me to shed real tears only before my canvases!

My wrinkles, my faded complexion will remain there, there my fluid soul will be imprinted for ever.


My town is dead. The Witebsk road is run!

All the family are dead.

I shall write a few words for myself alone.

You need not read them. Look away.

My sisters! It is dreadful not to have given father a gravestone yet, nor Rosine, nor David. Write to me at once, we'll agree on something. In the end, we'll forget where each one lies.

My memory is afire.

I made a sketch of you, David, with the mandolin in your hand. You were laughing. Your rosy mouth, showing all your teeth. You are blue in my picture.

You lie in the Crimea, in a foreign land, in that place you drew so painstakingly from your hospital window. My heart is with you.

My dear father . . .

The longing of our last years tears me apart, and my canvases quake with those blasts.

My father loaded lorries; he hardly earned his living.

A lorry knocked him down, ran over him, and killed him outright. Just like that.

They hid the letter announcing his death from me.

Why? For I hardly ever cry now. I did not go back to Witebsk.

So I did not see Mamma's death, nor Papa's.

I couldn't have borne it.

I already feel life too keenly. To see that "truth", too, with my own eyes . . . to lose the last illusion . . . I cannot.

But perhaps it would be good for me.

I ought to have seen the features of my parents in death, my mother's face, her dead face, utterly white — seen it with my own eyes.

She loved me so dearly. Where was I? Why didn't I come? It isn't right.

And my father's face, crushed by fate and by the wheels of a lorry. It's bad that I wasn't there. If I had appeared, he would have been so glad. But he will not come back to life.

I shall see your grave later. It is very close to Mamma's.

I shall lie down full length on your grave.

Even then, you will not come back to life.

And when I am old (or perhaps before) I shall lie down at your side.

Enough of Witebsk. It is finished.

A full-stop on its art.


Only you, you are with me. The only one of whom my soul will not speak a word in vain.

When I gaze at you, it is as if you were my own work.

More than once you have saved my canvases from a dismal fate.

I do not understand men, any more than my pictures. Everything you say is right. So guide my hand. Take the brush and, like the leader of an orchestra, carry me off to far and unknown realms.

May our late parents bless the conception of our painting. May black be more black and white even whiter.

And our little girl is with us. Forgive me, dear, for not remembering you sooner, for not coming to see you until four days after you were born.

It is shameful. I had hoped for a boy and it was the opposite.

# 17

Idotchka is born. Almost immediately after her birth, we took her to the country.

A newborn baby is not a fragile vase. My wife wrapped her up from her head to her toes, so that she shouldn't catch cold.

I told her: "I think you should uncover her mouth, at least. A living thing needs air."

At last we arrived. And the moment we undid that baby bundle, we screamed in unison with the child, who was red with anger and puffing like a volcano.

"You see?"

My sister and her husband were our neighbours. Their baby left a trail behind him at every step. So, all day long, the floor was stained. What about chamber-pots, then?

In the bedroom, a single window.

You could see a bit of road and a pine tree in the middle. But my brother-in-law sat down in front of it and blotted out the entire landscape.

Idotchka refused to take sugared water.

Drops of milk had become rare. They must have been very tasty, for although we hadn't sweetened her water, the cunning little thing could tell the difference.

She screamed so loud I couldn't stop myself throwing her furiously on to her bed.

"Shut up!"

I can't stand children's piercing screams. It's awful!

In a word, I am no father.

People will say I'm a monster.

I'm losing their respect.

What's the use of writing all this?

And later! Do you remember, my dear, what happened a few years later, in Malachowka?

I had a dream: a little dog bit our Idotchka. It was dark. Through the window of my room I could see the vault of the sky crossed by gigantic, multicoloured squares, radio-meters, circles, meridians, streaked with written signs.

Moscow, stop; Berlin, stop; New York, stop. Rembrandt, Witebsk. Millions of ordeals.

All the colours, except the ultramarine, burn and burn again.

I turn round and see my picture in which the men are beside themselves.

It was hot. Everything looked green.

I lie between those two worlds and look out of the window. The sky is no longer blue, and in the darkness it hums like a seashell and outshines the sun.

Could that dream have been related to my race across

the fields the following day, when my little girl fell down and hurt herself?

Screaming, blood pouring down the little stick that had pierced her cheek, she ran towards me with all her might.

And once more I feel everything twisting up inside me, I know I'm even walking over the ground in a strange way.

If I could write, the coils of my words would be duller than the earth in that field where you fell, my darling.

I feel that everything will be different after me.

And will this world be alive?

# 18

But my pupils have repented. They urge me to go back to my school. They have drawn up a petition, declaring that they need me.

They swear to obey me, etc.

So here I am again with my family, in a goods van, along with the pram, the samovar, and other household objects.

My soul, like a damp room, slowly perspires.

Hope is hidden in the leather portfolio.

There lies my judgment and the weight of all my illusions.

It is snowing. It's cold. No wood.

They have installed me in two rooms that form part of an apartment occupied by a large Polish family. Their glances pierced you like swords.

"Just you wait; the Poles will soon come to Witebsk and they'll kill your father," their children would tell my little girl.

In the meantime, the flies bombarded us.

We lived very near the barracks. Millions of flies swarmed out of them merrily, flying gaily down the street, finding their way into our rooms through every cranny.

They stung pictures, faces, arms, furniture, my wife and my child, until she fell ill.

Soldiers walk past our windows. Dirty ragged little boys play outside our doors, and my daughter, seized with pity, makes them a present of our silver spoons and forks.

I move house again. A rich old man ventures to take us in, in the hope that I as director of the School, will be able to protect him. From what?

In fact, they left him alone.

This miserly old recluse eats like a sick dog. His cook blows into the empty sauce-pans and smiles, waiting for him to die.

No-one goes into his house. Outside, there is the revolution. He has no idea of what is going on. He does nothing but look after his property.

He sits alone at his big table.

The hanging lamp, brilliant in his wife's lifetime, is hardly alight now, and its murky shadow silhouettes his bent shoulders, twisted arms, his beard, and his yellowish, wrinkled face.

He has nothing to do.

At night, when the soldiers of the Cheka came to search his house, they had to go through our room.

They stop to question me first.

I show my papers. They read them, smiling.

"And in there?"

"The old man who lives there is so old that he'll drop dead the moment you go in. Would you risk that?"

And they went away.

I saved him in that way more than once, until he died a natural death.

That was the end of my apartment. Where could I go?

My in-laws' house had been destroyed long before this.

One afternoon, seven of the Cheka's cars drew up in front of the dazzling shop-windows and soldiers began to pile the entire contents of the three shops into them — precious stones, gold, silver, and watches. They even went into the apartment to see if there was anything of value there.

They even took the kitchen silver which had only just been cleared from the table.

Then they marched up to my mother-in-law, thrusting their revolvers under her nose:

"The keys of the safe, or else . . .

Either because they didn't know how to open the safes, or because they respected their value, they laboriously loaded them into their cars too.

Then they left, satisfied.

My in-laws, suddenly aged, were left dumb, arms dangling, eyes staring towards the distant spot where the seven cars had disappeared.

The crowd that had gathered wept silently.

They had taken everything. There wasn't even a spoon left.

That evening, they send the maid out to look for some ordinary spoons.

The father takes his, puts it to his mouth, and sets it down. Tears run down the tin spoon and fall into his tea.

At nightfall, the Chekists came back, armed with guns and shovels.

"Search!"

With the aid of an "expert", an envious enemy, they made holes in the walls and ripped up the floorboards. They were looking for hidden treasures.

That was enough to break the spirit of my parents-in-law, although they were used to frequent disturbances and attacks by ordinary thieves, tempted by their all too evident wealth.


Moscow surrounded by the Kremlin, or the Kremlin surrounded by Moscow, by the Soviets.

Hungry mouths and the howling of October.

What am I? A writer or something?

Must I describe how our muscles hardened during those years?

The flesh turned into paints, the body into a brush, and the head into a lathe.

I put on my wide trousers, my yellow smock (gifts from Americans who took pity on us and sent us their old clothes), and I went to the meetings, like everyone else.

There were a great many.

A meeting on foreign policy chaired by Lunatcharsky; a theatrical meeting; poets' and artists' meetings.

Which should I choose?

Meyerhold, with a red scarf round his neck and the profile of an exiled emperor, is the bulwark of the theatrical revolution.

Not so very long ago, he was working at the Imperial Theatre, and flaunting the uniform.

He is the only one of them I like. I'm even sorry I never worked with him.

Poor Taïroff, so eager for novelties, which reach him third-hand. Meyerhold gave him no peace.

And there was no better entertainment than their frequent squabbles.

At the poets' meeting, Mayakowsky was the one who shouted the loudest.

Although he had written a dedication to me in one of his books: "God grant that everyone may *chagall** like Chagall!", we were not friends.

He knew that his shouting and spitting in public disgusted me.

Does poetry need so much noise?

I preferred Essenine, whose broad smile touched me.

He shouted too, intoxicated with God, not with wine.

With tears in his eyes, he would beat his breast, not the table, and spit on himself, not on other people.

He waved to me from the rostrum.

* 'Have walked' in Russian.

His poetry may not be perfect; but isn't it the only cry from the soul in Russia, apart from Blok's?

And what could I do at the painters' meeting?

There, yesterday's pupils, former friends and neighbours, control art through Russia.

They regard me with mistrust and pity.

But I have no pretensions left, and in any case, I am no longer in demand as a teacher.

Who isn't a teacher these days, except me?

Here's one of the leaders of the "Bubnowy Walet" group.

Pointing to a lamp-post in the middle of the Kremlin Square, he adds maliciously:

"That's where they'll hang the lot of you."

It seems that meanwhile, he's a very keen revolutionary.

Another man, whom God deprived of talent, raises the cry: "Down with painting!"

The "successful" artists of the Tzarist days glare at him resentfully.

In the distance I can see my old friend Tugendhold, who was one of the first to talk about me.

Now he is enamoured of proletarian art, and just as single-minded about that as he used to be about Western art.

A would-be artist talks patronizingly about painting, in his ignorance. Finally, gazing adoringly at a chair in front of him, he exclaims:

"Now, my wife and I will do nothing but paint chairs."

A new revelation, like the "discoveries" of Cubism, of Simultaneism, Constructivism, counter relief, which returned from Europe ten years later.

And they end by "revealing themselves" again in academism.

But when I heard someone shout: "I don't care a ... for your soul. I need your legs, not your head," I made up my mind.

Enough! I want to keep my soul.

And I think the Revolution can be great without giving up respect for other people.

Had I only been a little bolder, I could have obtained various privileges, like so many others. But no.

I'm a stammerer. I'm always scared.

I look for a room in Moscow. I've had enough of Witebsk.

In the end I found an attic overlooking the courtyard. Damp. The bedclothes harbour the damp. The baby sleeps in the damp. The pictures turn yellow. The walls seem to be dripping.

Am I in prison or something?

A bundle of wood is lying at the foot of the bed.

I had a job to get it.

"The wood's dry," the cunning peasant assured me. Where can I find someone to saw it up?

I couldn't possibly carry those great logs up to the fifth floor, and I wouldn't risk leaving them outside to be stolen.

With four soldiers, whom I met by chance, I dragged armfuls of wood up to our room, and stacked them crosswise, as if the room were a shed.

At nightfall you would have thought a whole forest had begun to thaw out. The pines drip and pour.

Are there wolves amongst those logs, foxes with long tails?

We felt as though we were sleeping out of doors, hearing the trickling of the water and melted snow.

All that was missing were the clouds of Moscow, and the moon.

Nevertheless, we slept and dreamed.

My wife woke up and asked me:

"Go and look at the baby. Is there much snow in her bed? Cover her mouth!"

No money. We didn't need any; there was nothing to buy.

I collect rations and drag them over the icy road, like a bundle of white wings mixed with raw, red bony meat.

What can we do with it? It's half a cow. A whole sack of flour – long live the mice!

I liked herrings, but herrings every day! I liked kasha made with millet. But every day!

Then we needed a bit of butter and some milk for the baby.

My wife takes her jewels to Soucharewska market, but the market is cordoned off, and the militia arrest her.

"For God's sake," she begs, "let me go. My baby is alone in the house. All I want to do is to exchange my rings for a quarter of butter."

I'm not complaining. I was all right. What did it matter?

A kind man took us into his apartment. We all slept in the same room – my wife, the child, the maid, and me.

The stove smokes. The pipes spit moisture into the beds. Tears of joy congeal in smoke-filled eyes. In one corner of the room the snow gleams like innocent cotton wool.

The wind blows softly and the crackling of the fire sounds, at a distance, like loud kisses.

We are cheerful and empty.

Smiles streak my face, and the black Soviet bread rumbles in my mouth, pierces my heart.

At night, our host gave shelter to two girls. That's how he consoled himself.

During a famine, in the days of the Soviets! You bourgeois!

In exasperation, I furiously attacked the floors and walls of the Moscow theatre.

My mural paintings sigh there, in obscurity. Have you seen them?

Rant and rave, my contemporaries!

In one way or another, my first theatrical alphabet gave you a belly-ache.

Not modest? I'll leave that to my grandmother; it bores me.

Despise me, if you like.

## 19

"There you are," said Effross, leading me into a dark room, "these walls are yours, you can do what you like with them."

It was a completely demolished apartment that had been abandoned by bourgeois refugees.

"You see," he continued, 'the benches for the audience will be here; the stage, there."

To tell the truth, all I could see there was the remains of a kitchen, and here . . .

"Down with the old theatre that stinks of garlic and sweat. Long live . . ."

And I flung myself at the walls.

The canvases were stretched out on the floor. Workmen, actors walked over them.

The rooms and corridors were in the process of being repaired; piles of shavings lay among my tubes of paint, my sketches. At every step one dislodged cigarette-ends, crusts of bread.

I was stretched out on the floor too.

I loved lying flat out on the ground like that at times. At home, they lay a dead man out on the ground. His nearest relatives, also on the ground, weep at his head.

I love lying on the ground like that, whispering my prayers and my sorrows to it.

I remember a distant ancestor of mine who did the paintings in Mohileff synagogue.

And I wept.

"Why didn't he call me to help him, a hundred years ago? At least let him pray now before the high altar, let him protect me.

"Pour one or two drops of eternal truth into me, my bearded grandfather."

To console myself, I sent Effroïm, the caretaker of theatre, to fetch me some bread and milk.

The milk wasn't real milk; the bread wasn't bread. Watery milk, with starch in it. Oatmeal bread the colour of tobacco, with straw in it.

Perhaps it was real milk from a Revolutionary cow. Or, more likely, the caretaker had simply filled the jug with water, mixed heaven knows what with it, and presented it to me like that, the wretch.

It was like white blood or even worse.

I ate, I drank, I blazed with anger.

I can still see that caretaker, the sole representative of the workers in our theatre.

His nose, his poverty, his cowardice, his stupidity, his

lice, which crawled over from him to me and back again.
Often he just stood there doing nothing and smiled
feverishly.

"What are you laughing at, idiot?"

"I don't know which to look at: your painting or you.
They're both so funny!"

Effroïm, where are you? You may have been no more
than a caretaker, but sometimes, by chance, you did stand
in front of the ticket office and even checked tickets.

I often thought: we ought to put him on the stage. Why
not? They took on the wife of the other caretaker.

That woman's figure reminded you of a block of damp
wood, covered with snow.

At rehearsals, she ranted and raved like a pregnant mare.

I wouldn't have wished the sight of her breasts on my
worst enemy.

Horrible!

Next door was the office of the director, Granowsky.
There wouldn't be much work for him until the theatre
was ready.

The room is narrow. He's in bed. On the floor, wood
shavings. He pampers his body.

"How are you, Alexei Michailowitch?"

He lies there and smiles, or he sulks and grumbles. He
often aims sharp words at me or at other visitors, masculine
and feminine alike.

I don't know if Granowsky is still smiling now.

But, like the milk Effroïm brought, his smile comforted
me a little.

I never dared ask him if he liked me.

So I left without finding out.

It had long been my dream to work for the theatre.

As early as 1911, Tugendhold had written somewhere
that the objects on my canvases were alive.

"I could have done psychological settings," he said.

I have thought about that.

Later on, he actually did advise the stage manager,

Taïroff, to bear me in mind for "The Merry Wives of Windsor".

We had a meeting with him, and we parted – that was all.

At the end of my stay in Witebsk, in 1919, after I had brought in arts and artists, friends and enemies, I was delighted to receive an invitation from Granowsky and Effross. They asked me to come and work for the opening of the new Jewish theatre.

It was Effross who insisted on inviting me.

Effross? Never-ending legs. Neither noisy, nor silent. He is alive. All movement, from left to right, from head to toe. Everything shines: his glasses, his beard.

He is here, there, and everywhere.

He's one of the friends I love, and he deserves it.

I heard of Granowsky for the first time in Petersburg, before the war.

A pupil of Rheinhardt's, he occasionally put on large-scale productions, which enjoyed a certain vogue after Rheinhardt's "Oedipus" visited Russia.

At the same time, he organized Jewish productions. His company was made up of men from every walk of life, with whom he founded his theatrical school.

I saw his productions, in the realistic style of Stanislavsky.

I did not conceal my dislike of them.

That was what worried me when I reached Moscow.

I felt that we would not agree, at least in the beginning.

I, always anxious and worried about the least thing; he, confident, given to mockery.

And – the main thing – not at all Chagall.

They asked me to paint the murals in the auditorium, and the scenery for the first production.

"Ah!" I thought, "here's an opportunity to shake up the old Jewish theatre, its psychological naturalism, its false beards. There, on the walls at least, I can let myself go and freely show everything I think necessary to the re-birth of the national theatre."

160

Hadn't I advised Michaëls, the actor, to have one of his eyes taken out to complete his make-up?

I set to work.

I painted a mural for the main wall: Introduction to the new national theatre.

The other interior walls, the ceiling and the friezes, depicted the forerunners of the contemporary actor – a popular musician, a wedding jester, a good woman dancing, a copyist of the Torah, the first poet dreamer, and finally a modern couple flying over the stage. The friezes were decorated with dishes and food, bagels and fruit, spread out on well-laid tables.

I looked forward to meeting the actors.

And I silently implored the stage manager, the actors, who passed me:

"Let us agree. Let's join forces and throw out all this old rubbish. Let's work a miracle!"

The actors liked me. They often sent me a piece of bread, or a drop of soup, a smile, or hope.

At that time, Granowsky was slowly moving beyond the renaissance of Rheinhardt and Stanislavsky towards new horizons.

And when I was there, he was still living in other worlds.

I don't know why he never took me into his confidence. I never dared confide in him, either.

The actor Michaëls – starving, like everyone else – was the one who broke the ice.

He came up to me more than once with his eyes and forehead bulging, his hair dishevelled. A short nose, thick lips. He follows your thoughts attentively, anticipates them and, by the acute angles of his arms and his body, jumps straight to the point. Unforgettable!

He gazed at my painting, begging me to lend him my sketches. He wanted to absorb them, familiarize himself with them, and try to understand them.

A month or two later, he announces gaily:

"I've studied your sketches, you know. I understood

161

them. The result is, I've completely changed my personality. Now I have a new way of using my body, of moving and speaking.

"Everyone looks at me," he says, "without realizing what's happened."

In answer, I smile. He smiles.

The other actors approach my canvases cautiously – as they approach me, perched on the tall ladder; they also try to see something, to understand.

Maybe they could change themselves too.

Everything was in short supply. No material for the costumes and sets.

The night before the theatre opened, people brought me old worn-out suits. I hurriedly painted them.

In the pockets I discovered cigarette-ends, crusts of bread.

On the eve of the opening, I couldn't even enter the auditorium, I was so spattered with paint. I even ran on to the stage a few seconds before the curtain went up to paint in the props. I couldn't stand "naturalism".

Suddenly there was a clash.

Granowsky hung up a real duster.

I sigh and shout:

"A real duster?"

"Who's stage manager here, you or me?" retorts Granowsky.

My poor heart!

Papa, Mamma!

Naturally, the first performance was not an artistic, whole, in my opinion.

But I felt that my task was finished.


Then the Habima theatre asked me to take on the setting for "The Dibbouk".

I didn't know what to do.

At that time, the two theatres were at war.

But I couldn't miss going to the "Habima", where the actors did not act but prayed, while they too, alas, praised Stanislavsky's dramatic art to the skies.

If our romance with Granowsky didn't "take", as he put it, I was even farther from Wachtangoff. Manager of the "Habima", he also acted in the Stanislavsky theatre, and his productions were still unknown at the time.

I thought it would be difficult for us to find a common language.

I respond to love, to the attachment of a like heart, but in the face of doubts, hesitancy, I retire.

When I went to the first rehearsals of "The Dibbouk" and listened to Wachtangoff, I thought: He's a Georgian. This is the first time we have met. He is silent. We examine each other awkwardly. No doubt he can read in my eyes the chaos and confusion of the East, an incomprehensible, foreign art.

"What's the use of worrying, blushing, and glaring at him? I'll inject a drop of poison into him.

"With me, or behind my back, he'll remember it one day. Others will follow me and translate my words and my sighs into a clearer, sharper, more popular form."

Then Zemach, the director of the "Habima", rouses me from my thoughts.

"Marc Zacharowitch, how do you think 'The Dibbouk' should be staged?"

"You'd better consult Wachtangoff first," I replied.

A pause.

Wachtangoff slowly replies that all these distortions mean nothing to him, that Stanislavsky's method is the only one.

I have rarely been so infuriated.

"In that case, why did you bother me?"

But I control myself and reply that I cannot see the place of that method in the renaissance of the Jewish theatre.

And, turning to Zemach:

"You will stage it my way all the same, even if I am not there! There's no other way."

Feeling better, I left.

On my way home, I recalled my first meeting with Ansky, the author of "The Dibbouk".

He caught sight of me during a reception, embraced me and told me happily:

"You know, I have a play, 'The Dibbouk'. You're the only one who can stage it. I've been thinking of you."

Baal-Machschowess, the writer, who was with us, nodded and said "yes" with his spectacles.

But what can I do?

It turned out, as someone told me afterwards, that a year later, Wachtangoff was spending hours in front of my murals in Granowsky's theatre (Zemach himself admitted it), and at the "Habima" they ordered another artist to paint "in the style of Chagall".

And I've also heard they go far beyond Chagall at Granowsky's now!

Well done!


While I was working in the theatre, I did not forget that my family was living in Malachowka, in a little country village near Moscow.

To reach it, I first had to stand in one queue for several hours to buy a ticket, then in another to get as far as the platform.

Wearing my smock and wide trousers, I couldn't do much to resist the pressure of the crowd.

Flocks of milkmaids banged their white tin churns mercilessly into my back. They trod on my feet. The peasants pushed.

Standing up or lying on the ground, they occupied themselves hunting lice.

Sunflower seeds cracked between their teeth and spurted out on my hands, my face.

At last, when the icy train slowly moved off at nightfall, the smoke-filled carriage rang with doleful or boisterous songs.

I felt as if I were ascending to heaven through birch-woods, snow, and clouds of smoke, with all those plump women, those bearded peasants, tirelessly making the sign of the cross.

Milk churns, empty of milk and full of money, rattled like drums.

Finally, the train stops and I get out. It's the same every day.

It is dark; I cross the deserted fields and I think I see a wolf crouching in the snow.

A wolf, definitely.

I turn aside, step back, and walk on cautiously, until I'm sure it's not a wolf. A poor dog lying motionless.

In the morning, I take the same road back to Moscow.

It is not yet day. The sky is lilac blue. The plain enfolds you in its thousands of miles. Joyful birches crown your head.

The flocks of milkmaids are on the platform again, with their churns of milky water; the same smelly peasants.

The goods train lumbers along, crackling with cold.

People run and collide as they rush towards the icy steps.

Suddenly, a piercing scream. A peasant woman who has fallen flat in the snow under the wheels of a carriage is shrieking wildly.

The violet blood from her broken leg is spreading over the snow.

"Oh! my brothers!" we hear her moan.

They dig, they shovel, they lift her up and carry her away, like so much manure.

We've seen all kinds.

# 20

The Narkompross* invites me to teach in the children's colony known as the "Third International", and also in the colony in Malachowka.

These colonies consisted of some fifty children, all orphans, cared for by clever teachers who dreamed of applying the most advanced teaching methods.

Those children were the most unhappy of orphans.

All of them had lately been thrown out on to the street, whipped by thieves, terrified by the flash of the dagger that cut their parents' throats. Deafened by the whistling of bullets and the crash of broken windows, they could still hear the last prayers of their fathers and mothers ringing in their ears. They had seen their father's beard savagely ripped off, their sisters disembowelled, hastily raped.

Ragged, shivering with cold and hunger, they roamed the towns, hung on to the buffers of trains until they were finally taken in to children's homes – a few thousand among so many others.

* Ministry of Public Education, in the Soviet Republic.

And here they are before me.

They lived in several different country houses, only coming together for their lessons.

In winter, their little houses were buried in snow, and the wind, raising clouds of snowflakes, whistled and sang in the chimneys.

The children were busy doing their housework, taking turns to prepare their meals, baking their bread, chopping and carrying their firewood, washing and mending.

They held meetings like men, deliberated, and passed judgment on one another, even on their teachers, and sang the International in chorus, with gestures and smiles.

I taught those poor little things art.

Barefoot, lightly clad, each shouted louder than the other, and cries of "Comrade Chagall! ..." rang out on all sides.

Only their eyes could not or would not smile.

I loved them. They drew pictures. They flung themselves at paints like wild beasts at meat.

One of those boys seemed to be in a perpetual frenzy of creation. He painted, wrote music and verses.

Another constructed his work quietly, like an engineer.

Some of them went in for abstract art, and verged on Cimabue and the art of stained-glass windows.

I continued to delight in their drawings, their inspired stammerings, until the moment I had to leave them.

What has become of you, my dears?

When I remember you, my heart aches.

They had given me an empty little wooden house so that I should be nearer the colony at Malachowka. However, it had a garret where we could live.

Our one iron bed was so narrow that by morning, our bodies were thoroughly battered and bruised.

We came across some trestles that we used to make our bed a bit wider.

That house still harboured the smell of its refugee owners, the suffocating atmosphere of contagious diseases.

167

Medicine bottles, the filth of domestic animals, lay about everywhere.

In summer and winter, the windows stayed wide open.

Downstairs, in the communal kitchen, a hilarious peasant woman did our housework.

As she put the bread in the oven, she would talk freely about her adventures, laughing and showing all her teeth:

"During the famine," she told us, "I used to come home on goods trains humping sacks of flour I somehow managed to pick up in distant parts of the country.

"Once, on the train," she went on, laughing, "I ran into a patrol of twenty-five militiamen. I was all by myself in the carriage.

"It's against the law to bring in flour," they say. "There's a new decree. Don't you know that?"

"Well! So I lay myself down. All twenty-five of them came, one after another. And I stayed put.

"In return, I brought back my sack of flour."

I looked her straight in the face.

At night, she went down to the ground floor where some forest guards were sleeping.

After a while, it was in her belly that she was carrying the bread. And she was living permanently with the forest guards.

I only hope they don't come up to our place, armed with their hatchets!


I am waiting patiently in the anteroom of the Narkompross until the head of the office deigns to see me.

I want, if possible, to get them to set a price for the murals I did for the theatre.

If they won't put them in the "first category" – which is easily managed by artists less adept than I – at least let them give me the minimum.

But the manager smiles.

"Yes ... yes ... you understand," he stammers, "the estimate ... the signatures, the seals ... Lunatcharksy. Come back tomorrow."

That went on for two years.

I got ... pneumonia. Granowsky smiled too.

What more could I do?

My God! Granted, you did give me talent, at least so they say. But why didn't you give me an impressive face, so that people would fear me and respect me? If I were stout, for example, majestically tall, with long legs, and a square head, then people would be overawed by me – that's the way of the world.

But my face is too mild. My voice has no ring to it.

I am in despair.

I trail about the streets of Moscow.

As I pass the Kremlin, I cast a furtive glance through the huge gates.

Trotsky gets out of his car; he is tall, his nose bluish-red. He strides boldly across the threshold and goes towards his apartment in the Kremlin.

An idea occurs to me: "Suppose I were to call on Demyan Bedny, the poet, who also lives in the Kremlin, and served on the Military Committee with me during the war?"

I'll enlist his aid, and Lunatcharsky's for permission to return to Paris.

I've had enough of being a teacher, a director.

I want to paint my pictures.

All my pre-war canvases are still in Berlin and Paris where my studio awaits me, full of sketches and unfinished pictures.

My good friend the poet Rubiner wrote from Germany:

"Are you alive? They say you were killed in the war.

"Do you know you are famous here? Your pictures have launched expressionism. They're fetching very good prices. Don't count on the money Walden owes you, all the same. He won't pay you, he maintains the glory is good enough."

Too bad.

I would rather think of my parents, of Rembrandt, my mother, Cézanne, my grandfather, my wife.

I would have gone to Holland, to the south of Italy, to Provence, and, stripping off my clothes, I would have said:

"You see, my friends, I've come back to you. I'm unhappy here. The only thing I want is to paint pictures, and something more."

Neither Imperial Russia nor Soviet Russia needs me.

I am a mystery, a stranger, to them.

I'm certain Rembrandt loves me.

## 21

These pages have the same meaning as a painted surface.

If there were a hiding place in my pictures, I would slip them into it ... Or perhaps they would stick on to the back of one of my characters or maybe on to the trousers of the "Musician" in my mural ... ?

Who can tell what's written on his back?

In the age of the R.S.F.S.R., I keep shouting:

Can't you feel our electric scaffoldings slipping under our feet?

And weren't our artistic premonitions right – since we really are up in the air and suffer from one disease alone: the thirst for stability.

Those five years churn in my soul.

I have grown thin. I'm even hungry.

I long to see you again, B. . . , C. . . , P. . . , I am tired.

And perhaps Europe will love me and, with her, my Russia.

*Moscow, 1922*